Other books by Will Manley

Snowballs in the Bookdrop
(1982)

Unintellectual Freedoms
(McFarland, 1991)

Other book by Gary Handman

Bibliotoons
(McFarland, 1990)

Other book by Manley and Handman

Unsolicited Advice
(McFarland, 1992)

UNPROFESSIONAL BEHAVIOR

Confessions of a Public Librarian

by Will Manley

Illustrations by Gary Handman

McFarland & Company, Inc., Publishers
Jefferson, North Carolina, and London

For Lorraine

British Library Cataloguing-in-Publication data are available

Library of Congress Cataloguing-in-Publication Data

Manley, Will, 1949–
    Unprofessional behavior : confessions of a public librarian / by
Will Manley ; illustrations by Gary Handman.
      p. cm.
    Includes index.
    ISBN 0-89950-690-9 (lib. bdg. : 50# alk. paper) ∞
    1. Manley, Will, 1949– . 2. Library administrators–United
States–Biography.   3. Public librarians–United States–Biography.
4. Books and reading–United States.   5. Public libraries–United
States. I. Handman, Gary, 1950–   . II. Title.
Z720.M34A3 1992
020'.92–dc20
[B]   91-40350
                                                       CIP

Manufactured in the United States of America

McFarland & Company, Inc., Publishers
  Box 611, Jefferson, North Carolina 28640

TABLE OF CONTENTS

Attention circulation clerks, junior librarians, senior librarians, library aides, library assistants, reference librarians, children's librarians, library janitors, library supervisors, library directors, and catalogers (especially catalogers):

The book is about unprofessional behavior — breaking the rules and, as Frank Sinatra would say, doing things your way.

Let's start at the beginning. What is the number one rule of librarianship? Right — *Every book must be cataloged, classified, pocketed, stamped, embossed, and jacketed.* That's rule numero uno.

What is rule number two? Right — after we've totally mauled a book by stamping it, embossing it, pocketing it, and jacketing it, we tell people to *Never damage or deface a library book.*

Neither rule applies to this book. The main reason I wrote this book was for therapy, mainly for me but also for hundreds and thousands of librarians like me.

We librarians are not the most respected people in the world. It seems like everyone from Hollywood to Madison Avenue likes to poke fun at our serious, fussbudget ways. So what do we do in response? Instead of laughing off our stereotype, we get overly defensive about it. We demand to be taken seriously. We demand to be respected as professionals. But there's an irony here. The more we try to act the part of the serious professional the more we reinforce our image of being stuffy, fussy, and stern. We need to stop taking ourselves and our image so seriously. A little relaxation is in order. That's what this book is supposed to do — help librarians lighten up.

If you've always wanted to scream at the top of your lungs in the library during the middle of the day, if you've always wanted to purposely put a book in a place not prescribed by Dewey, if you've always wanted to tell an unreasonable patron to take a flying leap, and if you've always wanted to tell a book censor what you thought of him or her in very uncensored language, you might enjoy this book. I've done many of these things, and I'm still around. Take it from me, professionalism is not everything.

In my opinion, librarianship is an overly normative pursuit. Things in our profession are just too carefully prescribed, regulated, and standardized. What's worse is the fact that we've convinced ourselves that we all have to follow these norms, practices, and principles to a tee. Unfortunately, in the process creativity has been sacrificed to conformity.

Enough already. Trying to be the perfect professionals in a most decidedly imperfect world causes us nothing but grief, depression, and ulcers. We need to learn how to enjoy the unexpected, the unpredictable, and yes, even the unprofessional aspects of our jobs. These are the things that make librarianship worth enduring. Wouldn't it be utterly awful to have a job in a highly respected profession like law or finance and be bored stiff all day? After working in the library field, do you really think you could stomach the humdrum routine that an accountant or a lawyer is faced with?

Of course you couldn't. You'd miss those favorite problem patrons of yours in a minute. The thing to do then is to stop worrying and learn to enjoy the follies of librarianship. Don't be constantly concerned about the precision of your added entries or the comprehensiveness of your bibliographic tracings. The world will never be as perfect and as orderly as you want it to be. So you can stop trying to be perfect yourself.

As I said, this book is about unprofessional behavior—breaking the rules and living to talk about it. The first thing I want you to do with this book, therefore, is to do nothing. Remember rule number one— that all books have to be *Cataloged, classified, embossed, stamped, pocketed, and jacketed.* Don't do any of those things to this book. Leave this book alone for goodness' sake. Don't put a bibliographic straitjacket on it. Let it live. Let it breathe. The fate of this book is completely in your hands.

So catalogers, when this book comes over from acquisitions, please just relax. Instead of searching for bibliographic records, sit back and pour yourself a nice cup of tea. Then browse through the book leisurely. It's okay, you're allowed to read some of it. One of the chapters is even about you. I hope you like what I had to say about you.

And if you enjoy the book, do something even more unprofessional. Break rule number 3 *(It is totally forbidden for anyone to remove any uncataloged materials from the cataloging workroom).* That's right, if you like this book, break rule number three and *Take it home.*

Then when you finish with it, pass it on to your colleagues with the understanding that they will read it and then pass it on to their colleagues. Make sure everyone who works at the library (don't forget the janitor) gets a crack at the book. It really bugs me that "nonprofessional" people never get their names on interdepartmental routing slips.

And when all of you get the book and take it home, be sure that you break rule number 2 *(Never damage or deface a library book).* Enjoy the book like it belongs to you. Don't treat it like a library book. Have you ever noticed how difficult it is to really enjoy a library book? You're always so afraid of bending the pages or breaking the spine that you just can't relax with it. But with your own book it's a different story. You don't have to worry about spilling food on it or falling asleep on top of it, or even getting it a little wet.

Books are actually very personal items. To really enjoy a book you've got to be able to get close to it—to sleep with it, eat with it, cuddle it, cradle it, scream at it, and even throw it. You can't do that with a library book. Spending time with your own book is like spending time with someone in your immediate family—it's informal, relaxed, and comfortable. Spending time with a library book is like spending time with a distant relative—it's stilted, awkward, and uncomfortable.

One of my favorite activities is going to used book sales because that's a surefire way to find a good book to read. As a librarian, I know that if you want to read a good book, the professional thing to do is consult the professional literature for book reviews. Sometimes this is helpful, but many times it's not. Book reviewers often have their own agendas that may not have anything to do with your own needs and wants. And they might have radically different standards, expectations, and perspectives from you. There's one other thing about book reviewers that you ought to consider—if they're so smart why are they writing book reviews instead of books?

No, never trust a book reviewer, not completely anyway. If you really want an effective method for finding a good book to read, go to a used book sale and look for the books with the most food stains on them. These books were so good that their readers could not put them down even while eating.

Once you have located these books, closely examine the stains. Pick out the book with the greatest variety. This will be the best book of the bunch. Look closely. Does the book have egg stains, coffee stains, ketchup stains, mayonnaise stains, and ice cream stains? Now smell the book. Does it smell of onions and relish? If you can answer yes to both questions you've got yourself a gem. All those clues tell you that the book was so good that the original owner read it straight through breakfast, lunch, or dinner.

Most of the time you won't get this lucky. You'll have to hunt for other clues. Books that have copious margin notes are usually very thought provoking. It's fun to read these books because of the bonus effect—you get to read both the original text and some other reader's reaction to it.

A book with water spots is one that bears further scrutiny because they may mean that the book was so good that someone could not take a bath without it. Check for fragances of bubble bath or bath oil. They are usually signs of a good romantic book.

Books with broken spines and pages falling out can also be quite promising. Oftentimes these are signs that a person has read and reread the book many times. Only really good books get read a lot. So the more wear and tear the better.

There are some books, on the other hand, that you should definitely stay away from. Books with large chunks of text highlighted in the annoying day-glo colors of lime green, neon orange, and mellow yellow should be avoided at all costs. They are obviously used college texts. This means only one thing—boring.

Books in which the upper right or left hand corner of every second, third, or fourth pages is folded should also be rejected. The presence of numerous folded page corners signifies that the book is so bad that the reader had to put it down every five minutes and marked his place by folding over the corner of the page he was on.

But, of course, the one book that you most definitely want to stay away from completely and forever is the book that looks too perfect. This is a book that is so bad that it has never been read. If the spine is not cracked, if the dust jacket is in mint condition, and if the page edges are not worn, put down this book immediately. It is even too boring to open up and browse through.

Now what I want you to do is walk over to the nonfiction stacks in your library and look through the books on library science. I have no doubt that most of these books will fit into the later category— unmussed, unwrinkled, and unread. That's what I am trying to avoid with this book. My fellow librarians, I beg of you to do me an unprofessional favor. Please keep this book away from your shelves. I do not want it to die an immediate death.

Catalogers, you can break the rules just this once. Take the book home, spill some mustard on it, take a bath with it, sleep with it, and then pass it on to the next guy. In fact, I wouldn't be at all opposed to having you rip the book apart and give different chunks of it to different people on the staff.

After all we are talking about unprofessional therapy here. We are interested in breaking a few taboos, aren't we? What could be more daring for a librarian than to take a brand new book and rip whole chapters out of it. Or you could use a razor blade like all the major library book thieves do. Then put routing slips on what you've ripped out and distribute it around to the staff. That's it, catalogers, you get to decide which chapters are most appropriate for which staff members. That way my book will get the widest possible exposure.

And if what you read doesn't entertain you or satisfy you or if you violently disagree with it then keep on ripping. Rip the pages up and use them for confetti. Remember, the worth of a book is in its use, and so I'd much prefer to have my book used for confetti or for kindling than to sit silently on a lonely library shelf.

If you want you could even call me to complain. I can be reached most weekdays at 602-350-5305 between 8 a.m. and 5 p.m. MST. I would be happy to hear from you but since I don't accept collect calls you might want to drop me a line at Tempe Public Library, 3500 S. Rural Rd., Tempe AZ 85282.

Happy ripping and happy reading.

IT NEVER RAINS IN SUNNY ARIZONA

The worst part of being a library director is the first day. No, that's not quite right. The whole first month is actually pretty awful. Better make that the entire first year. I should know. I've directed three different libraries, and in each case the first year was less fun that a flat tire on the freeway. A lot less fun.

First, there's the matter of the build-up. Your library board has one basic purpose in life — to hire a library director. Everything else that the board does is secondary to that. So naturally when the board hires a new library director it wants to create the impression that it has just hired the greatest librarian in history, correct that — the greatest human being in history.

That's what you discover when you sit down at your office desk for the first time. There on top of your brand new appointment calendar is a newspaper clipping about you. It starts out with a quote from the chairman of the search committee. "After conducting a very thorough and very competitive selection process, we feel that we have come up with the perfect individual to direct our public library." That's just the beginning. The article goes on to say that you can heal the sick and walk on water. Admittedly, the tone of the article is partially your own fault. After all, in your eagerness to get the job, you're the one who told the search committee that you had miraculous powers.

All eyes will, therefore, be upon you to catch a glimpse of your magic. The library staff will be especially attentive to how well you measure up to your advance notices. The painful reality, of course, is that in the early days of a new directorship you know less about the library than the lowliest janitor. While everybody assumes that you are going to be an instant and abundant source of organizational illumination, the truth is that you're just a desperate guy groping around in the dark trying to find the light switches.

The key, of course, is to create the impression that you really are the miracle worker that everyone is anticipating. By all means, you must mask your ignorance and insecurities under a calm exterior of sincerity, friendliness, and professionalism. On the outside you must radiate confidence even though on the inside you are quivering like a jellyfish. All those clichés about first impressions are true. This doesn't mean you have to go around walking on water, it just means that you should give the impression that you could walk on water if the need ever arose.

Therefore, when the Head of Cataloging approaches you and complains that there is a backlog of over 5,000 titles, you should say with complete conviction: "I have a definite idea about how to get that situation cleaned up." Just don't tell her that your idea is to back up an industrial sized dumpster to the cataloging room and throw the entire mess away. Likewise, when the Head of Circulation approaches you and says that because the library has spent two million dollars on a dysfunctional computer system it takes ninety seconds just to check out one book, tell her: "I have a definite idea about how to significantly increase response time." Just don't tell her that your idea is to implement a phantom check-out system by which you simply run a laser wand over a book without even bothering to turn the computer on.

The successful new library director is an expert tap dancer who knows how to do nothing in a very, very impressive way. The key is to create the illusion that you are actively doing something about the library's many problems while in reality you are trying to figure out where all the organizational skeletons are buried. Before you do anything you need to find out for yourself who you can trust and who you can't. While you are publicly advancing your image as the guy with all the answers, you are privately learning the idiosyncrasies of the organization.

This is a difficult charade to play because most libraries that get new directors are rife with problems that cry out for immediate attention. New directors usually inherit one of two situations. They have to replace either a legend or a loser. I'm not sure which scenario is more difficult.

The legend is the director who has finally retired after decades of service. Most, if not all, of the existing staff was hired by the legend, and the current library building was probably designed and built by him. The problem is that after hiring the staff and building the building, the legend did little else. In fact he probably cruised through the last ten or fifteen years of his reign on automatic pilot. Consequently, the quality of services declined, the library's technological base became obsolete, the budget did not keep pace with inflation, and the collection became dated. In this scenario, the new director is expected to right all the wrongs of the last fifteen years with one wave of his magic wand.

Replacing a loser is equally problematic. The loser is the library director who was fired after a relatively short and stressful run. He was probably canned for one of the following reasons: failure to get along with the staff, failure to get along with the board, failure to get along with the City Council, or failure to get along with the community. Ninety-nine percent of the library directors who get the sack, fail because of their inability to unify people behind a common goal. They tend to drive people apart rather than bring them together. Therefore, when you replace a loser you usually find yourself in the middle of an organizational war. The board members may hate each other and the staff may be split into warring factions, but you are expected to miraculously usher in a golden age of wholeness and healing.

In order to maintain everyone's initial confidence in you, it is absolutely essential to score some early victories. The best strategy is to pick a battle that you know you can win quickly and clearly. Don't bend your pick on an issue that defies a quick fix. Tackling the cataloging backlog during your first week is only asking for trouble. You'll end up getting bogged down in a quagmire of philosophical differences, staff skirmishes, and computer glitches. It's much more advisable to tackle something clean and simple – like a leaky roof.

When I got to the Tempe Public Library as its new library director, I walked into one of the most dysfunctional public organizations I had ever seen. The staff was divided into cliques and the board was quite quarrelsome. The overall atmosphere was filled with fear, insecurity, and mistrust. "Don't ever turn your back on anybody!" is what one of the veteran librarians told me. The situation screamed out for an organizational messiah who could lead the library into the promised land of trust, cohesiveness, and cooperation.

The first thing I did was sit down at my desk and read the newspaper clipping that proclaimed that I was going to be that messiah. Then, inspired by the references in the article to my ability to walk on water and make the blind see, I decided to go for a stroll around my new library. What I saw in this beautiful ten-year-old building was an irregular pattern of wastebaskets all over the public services area. They were placed in the most illogical locations – in the middle of the bookstack aisles, in front of the circulation desk, and even on top of some of the study tables.

Curious, I asked one of the librarians at the reference desk about the wastebaskets. "Oh, it's the roof," she said. "It's leaked like a vegetable strainer for several months."

"Why doesn't anyone fix it?" I asked.

"Because no one seems to be able to get anyone out here," she said shaking her head. We've all gotten used to the wastebaskets. They sort of do the job. That and the fact that it never rains here in sunny Arizona."

I was both appalled and excited. Appalled because nothing had been done to fix the leaky roof and excited because nothing had been done to fix the leaky roof. Here was my opportunity to get something done quickly that no one else had been able to get done.

I talked to a few more staff members about the roof and pretty soon the library grapevine was buzzing with rumors that "Manley actually thinks he can get the roof fixed." I even overheard one person saying, "If Manley can do that, he can do anything."

This kind of incentive was all I needed. I rushed over to my secretary's work station. "Who is in charge of building maintenance?" I demanded.

"Charlie Snider," she said smiling.

"Please get him on the phone right away."

Several seconds later, Snider was on the phone. "Mr. Snider," I said, "this is Will Manley. I'm the new library director.

"Welcome to Tempe," he said cheerfully. "What can I do for you?"

"I'm calling about the library roof," I said. "It leaks like a vegetable strainer."

"Right," he said, "it needs to be replaced."

"Good!" I exclaimed, "when will the work be done?"

"Next year," he said politely. "It's not budgeted this year."

"NEXT YEAR!" I screamed hoping that I could convince Mr. Snider that I was not a wimp.

"Yeah, that's right," he replied casually. "A roof like that costs fifty thousand dollars. I just don't have it budgeted. But don't worry, it never rains here in sunny Arizona."

"MR. SNIDER," I screamed, "I'M VERY DISAPPOINTED WITH YOUR ATTITUDE. DO YOU REALIZE HOW ABSURD THIS SITUATION IS? ACCORDING TO MY STAFF, EVERY TIME IT RAINS NEW LEAKS APPEAR AND GUESS WHAT? WE'RE OUT OF WASTEBASKETS. THE NEXT TIME IT RAINS WE'RE GOING TO HAVE WATER ALL OVER EVERYTHING — THE BOOKS, THE CARPETING, AND ALL THE FURNITURE. SOMETHING MUST BE DONE ABOUT THIS IMMEDIATELY. IF YOU DON'T ADDRESS THIS PROBLEM SOON I'M GOING TO REPORT YOU TO THE CITY MANAGER. DO YOU UNDERSTAND ME?"

"Okay, okay," said Snider nervously. "I see your point. I'll take care of the situation first thing tomorrow morning."

"You will?" I asked incredulously.

"Yeah," he said, "I'll be there first thing in the morning."

"Thank you, Mr. Snider. It's public servants like yourself who make Tempe such a great place to work."

I hung up the phone and called the secretary into my office. "I want you to call together a short staff meeting right away."

Two hours later in front of the entire staff I made my announcement. "Ladies and gentlemen," I said very, very self-importantly, "I just want you all to be the first to know what a little perseverance and friendly persuasion can do. I have prevailed upon Mr. Charlie Snider to take care of our roof problem tomorrow."

Although a few of the staffers applauded my announcement with enthusiasm, there were others who remained skeptical. One reference librarian even muttered, "I'll believe it when I see it." I shot this person a very ungrateful look. I had called this meeting to glory in congratulations. It was not my intention to be beset with doubt. "A little positive thinking could do some of you a world of good," was the statement with which I concluded the meeting. It simply generated more sarcasm. "You don't know Charlie Snider," was the last comment I heard.

The next day I was late getting to my office because of an early morning meeting that I had to attend at City Hall. When I arrived at the library I rushed over to one of the catalogers. "Has Mr. Snider been here?" I asked.

"Oh, yes," she said smiling. "He sure has." She started laughing. I didn't like the sound of her laughter. It had a nervous edge to it.

"Why are you laughing?" I asked cautiously.

"Go look in you office," she said trying very hard to keep a straight face. "Mr. Snider left you some things."

I rushed over to my office. It seemed like the entire staff followed me. I wondered what the big deal was. I opened the door. There in a nice neat stack were ten brand new thirty-gallon wastebaskets with a note from Mr. Snider. "These should last you for the entire year."

I could hear one of the staff members mumble, "He sure took care of that problem, didn't he." Everyone giggled nervously.

I looked up at everyone and said, "So what? It never rains in sunny Arizona."

And that's a good thing because I can't walk on water.

ACCOUNTABILITY

I've noticed that lately there's been a lot written about new trends in "starting a family." Apparently today's young professionals want it all. They want the house, the boat, the four-wheel drive, and the time share in the Bahamas. Then and only then is it time to start talking about a baby. I have to assume that's why so many couples are waiting until they are in their late thirties or early forties to start a family. It takes time to buy a house, a boat, a four-wheel, and a time share in the Bahamas. I suppose that's a nice approach if you can do it that way. I never could. My kids entered the world according to their plans, not mine.

But somehow I know there's got to be a dark side to the house–boat–four-wheel–time share–baby scenario. After all that plotting and planning I really wonder what happens to the parents once the baby arrives. You can do all the preparing and scheduling you want before the child is born but the harsh reality is that babies bring utter, absolute chaos after they arrive. Once a baby is born you can say good-bye forever to your life of rational decisionmaking. That image created by Hallmark cards that parenthood is bliss and that children are a perpetual source of love, happiness, and satisfaction is complete balderdash.

Actually "family planning" is one of those dangerous oxymorons that people take all too seriously. The planning stops abruptly at childbirth. From there on it's a free-for-all beginning with midnight feedings and early morning colic attacks and continuing right on through to the trauma of driver's licenses and teen dating. Maybe I'm warped but whenever I see a newborn child I automatically think that in fifteen years and 364 days that kid will be driving a car.

The key word for surviving parenthood is not "planning." It is "temporary insanity" (twenty years of temporary). Who can plan for the time when your kid throws up fifty times on a simple two hour car trip to the state park? Who can plan for the day when your neighbor calls and complains that your child has tipped over his Christmas tree and broken a valuable vase? Who can plan for the evening when your child calls up and says that he's wrecked your car on the freeway and wonders if he might borrow your other car for the night?

The point is don't let children into your life if you're not ready for the prospect of going two entire decades without a totally sound sleep. As a parent what you quickly learn is to forget about idealistic concepts like pride and dignity and to concentrate on more realistic goals like survival. If after twenty years your child is not a drug addict, not a high school drop-out, and not in jail, you've done your job. Be thankful for life's modest blessings.

The problem with today's yuppie parents is that they expect too much from their kids. Having meticulously planned every detail for the child's birth (down to the angle of the video camera), they expect to plan the child's life in much the same way. This causes problems. Children have a natural affinity for freedom. The parent who expects to dictate the child's every move will inevitably crash head on into that quest for freedom.

More and more the biggest challenge of children's librarianship is dealing with unreasonable parents. It shouldn't be that way. The library, of all places, provides a welcome haven for children. It is a perfect place to give their affinity for freedom a free rein. It is a place where children can escape the pressures of teachers, parents, and principals and follow the yellow brick road of books wherever they so desire.

Think about it. We librarians are the only people who trust children enough to give them their own credit cards. This trust means something to kids. It means that we care about them and that we welcome them with all their enthusiasm even if at times that enthusiasm can take us to the very edge of our patience.

Our work to nurture, encourage, and challenge young readers, unfortunately, can conflict with parents who want to control how their children use the library. To the mothers and fathers who say to their children: "Read this, don't read that"; "You can only check out three books at a time"; and "You have only three minutes to look for books, we're late for your violin lessons", we want to scream in return: "LEAVE THE KID ALONE!"

The most formidable problem parent that I have ever run into was Ms. Judith Timkins-Halsey. She was a tax accountant. Her husband was a mechanical engineer. How Ms. Timkins-Halsey and her husband ever found time to have their daughter Amy I'm not quite sure. But they did, and all of us on the library staff were quite glad that they did. Amy was our favorite patron. We first became aware of her during our summer reading program. She had just completed the first grade and as is the case with many beginning readers she simply could not get enough books to read.

Exactly once a week during the summer Ms. Timkins-Halsey

would allow Amy to roam freely through the Children's Library for an entire afternoon, and at the end of that afternoon Amy would leave with as many books as she could haul out to the parking lot. Unfortunately Amy never seemed to come back with as many books as she left with. One month into the summer reading program we were fully aware that Amy had an acute overdue problem.

How did we know this? Her mother let us know in very direct terms.

"How can you continue to allow Amy to check out books?" Ms. Timkins-Halsey asked me over the phone one day. "She has out numerous overdue books and several unpaid fines. Don't you people believe in accountability?"

"Let's not lose sight of what's important," I said. "An overdue problem is not exactly grand theft. We wouldn't want a few unpaid fines to get in the way of a child's reading development."

"I don't approve of that kind of permissiveness," replied Ms. Timkins-Halsey, the tax accountant. "Amy needs to understand the principles of accountability."

A week later I had an opportunity to see Ms. T.-H. in person. She had decided to come to the library to make sure that Amy write down the title of every book that she checked out. "Next week," Mrs. Timkins-Halsey said to our circ clerk, "I want you to put a check through every book that Amy returns. She is not allowed to check out anymore books until all the books on this list are returned. She must learn accountability."

"Okay," said the circ clerk, shrugging her shoulders.

Next week rolled around and Amy only brought back five of the eleven books that she had checked out the previous week. "What should I do?" the circ clerk asked me.

I looked down at Amy's big brown eyes and said, "There is no way we are going to prohibit Amy from checking out more books. She has rights. This library does not have two circulation policies—one for Ms. Timkins-Halsey and one for everybody else. Let Amy check out whatever she wants."

Two weeks later Ms. T.-H. called. "Mr. Manley," she said, "I am tired of receiving overdue notices in my mailbox. Apparently you have decided not to enforce the rules I set for Amy. Therefore, I am giving you forewarning. If Amy gets one more overdue notice, I am going to take her library card and cut it into little pieces. I happen to know that it is the policy of your library not to check out books to people who do not have a library card, and I trust that you will not violate your own rules."

"Ms. Timkins-Halsey," I pleaded, "if the problem is money we can put Amy on the installment plan."

"Mr. Manley, I am quite offended that you would suggest that the problem is money. I happen to be a certified public accountant and my husband happens to be a highly respected mechanical engineer. We have a nice home, a fourteen foot cabin cruiser, a Jeep Cherokee, and a time share arrangement in the Bahamas. I assure you that the issue is not money. The issue, Mr. Manley, is accountability."

I quickly alerted the circ staff and the children's staff. "We must somehow help Amy. One more overdue and Ms. T.-H. takes the scissors to her card."

"That's child abuse," said one of the librarians.

"I agree," I said, "but tell that to Amy's mother."

So everytime Amy came to the library we coached her, cajoled her, and even tied a string around her finger for every book that she checked out. And I'll be honest. There were a few times we even cheated a little for her. But by the end of the summer, this little girl, who had the most voracious reading appetite of any child I have ever encountered, had learned enough about the principle of accountability to teach us something about the subject.

One hot August day, in front of about seventy-five patrons, Amy bounded enthusiastically up to the circulation desk and slammed down three books onto the counter with great excitement. Then in a loud and boastful voice she declared, "THESE BOOKS ARE A DAY EARLY. YOU OWE ME FIFTEEN CENTS!"

Knowing that Amy was a special case because of her mother, the circ clerk looked over to me for guidance. "What should I do?" she asked.

Without hesitation I answered, "GIVE HER THE MONEY!" and then I turned to everyone in the library and said, "THAT'S ACCOUNT-ABILITY."

It was a busy day. Correct that. It was a very busy day. I was knee deep in papers, meetings, and stress. The roof was leaking, my revised budget figures were due at City Hall in thirty minutes, I had to prepare for a library board meeting that evening, and I had just received word that some shady character with an eye-patch had checked out three hundred books from the bookmobile.

The phone rang. Craddling the receiver against my shoulder I continued to compute my budget figures. "Mr. Manley?" asked a woman with a very concerned voice.

"Yes."

"Hello."

"Hello. What can I do for you today?"

"I have a problem with a book."

"An overdue?"

"No, it's not overdue."

"Oh."

"It's *Where Did I Come From*."

"What?" I asked, very confused. "It makes no difference to me where you came from."

"*Where Did I Come From* is the title of the book. It's a children's book" she explained.

"Oh," I said. "I'm sorry but that title just doesn't ring a bell with me. What's the problem?"

"The man's thing."

"What?" I asked confused again.

"The size of the man's thing," she said.

"What thing?" I asked.

"You know," she said, "a certain part of his body."

"No, I don't know," I said trying hard to picture a man with a tuba sized head or elephant sized ears. I've seen some pretty crazy children's books over the years.

"I have a problem with the size of a certain body appendage," she said.

"What appendage?" I asked trying to imagine a foot long thumb. I remembered reading one children's book that featured a pig with a nose shaped like a two liter coke bottle.

"A certain body appendage on the man."

"What man?"

"The man in the book."

"Oh," I said deciding to put down my budget figures and devote all my attention to this incoherent caller. "I really am not familiar with the book."

"Well, I checked out the book yesterday to read to my daughter and I was horrified to see the size of this man's body part. It could frighten a young girl. Please look at the book and see for yourself. I'd rather not talk about it anymore. Just turn to page nine and you will see what I mean."

"Thank you for your concern," I said relieved to finally bring this conversation to a close. When I get a moment I will go down to the children's library, look at the book, check the reviews of the book, consult with my children's librarian about the book, and then when I can talk knowledgeably about the book I'll call you back."

"Thank you very much, Mr. Manley. Just be sure and check page nine."

"Thanks again for calling. Goodbye."

"Goodbye, Mr. Manley."

I hung up the phone and started scrutinizing the budget again. But I couldn't concentrate. I kept thinking about the woman's complaint. What could be so horrible about the character in this children's book that it would frighten a young girl. I pictured a monstrous old ogre with oversized teeth and a patch over his eye. Unable to concentrate on the budget, I hurried down to the children's room to get the book.

Fortunately, there was a copy of it on the shelves. Not wasting any time I turned right to page nine. There in full frontal nudity stood a comical, bald headed, fat, little cartoon figure. I looked closely but could find nothing about this little guy that was inappropriately large. What could this woman be talking about? I browsed quickly through the entire book. Maybe she was objecting to the subject matter. The book was a sex education primer for children.

To check on my own sanity I showed the offending page to a number of people on staff. No one saw anything that was inappropriately large on the man's body. Finally someone said "Isn't the man's penis a little exaggerated in size? Not much, but a little?" This initiated a very embarrassing debate among several staffers that I did not wish to be a part of. Plus I had work to do.

My unprofessional strategy in this case was to stall. There was no way I wanted to get into a debate with anyone on the size of this cartoon figure's body part. I do try to maintain a certain level of dignity in my life. My sincere hope was that the concerned parent would not call back.

She called back two days later. "What was your reaction to the book?" she asked.

"I've looked at the book," I answered, "but quite frankly I haven't had an opportunity to look up the book reviews."

"Oh, that's not necessary," she replied. "The quality of the book is not the issue here."

"What is the issue?" I asked.

"The size of the man's body part," she said.

"Well, in that case, I'd say that I really don't think that there's anything objectionable."

"You don't think that the man's body part is too big?"

"No, no, I don't?"

"You don't think that the size of the man's body part would frighten a young girl?"

"No, no I don't."

"I can't believe that you would say that," she muttered with frustration.

"Let me get this straight," I said with my own frustration, "are you talking about the p word?"

"YES, I'M TALKING ABOUT THE P WORD!"

"Then I can only give you my opinion, and my opinion is that it is not too big. Maybe the reviewers see it differently, but like I said I haven't had time to look up the reviews."

"I don't care what you say, I think it's too big!"

"That's your opinion," I countered. "I have been in many locker-rooms and I would have to say that based on my observations the man's body part is big, but not unrealistically big."

"Have you seen bigger?" she asked with genuine curiosity.

"Yes," I answered, "I would have to say that I have seen bigger."

"I take it that your final decision is to keep the book in the collection?" she asked.

"Yes," I said.

"In that case could you at least put a warning label on the cover of the book that asks parents to look at page nine before they check the book out for their children?"

"No, I can't," I said. "Labeling violates the American Library Association's Library Bill of Rights."

"Well if you're not even willing to compromise, I must appeal your decision to a higher level."

"Fine," I said, "your next recourse is to appear in person at the next library board meeting to argue your case."

"That's out of the question!" she exclaimed. "My husband would never allow me to do that! I shouldn't have to appear in public to discuss such an embarrassing thing!" Then she slammed down the phone in a huff.

I never heard from her again. But I'm honestly sorry she decided not to appear before the board. I've been to some interesting board meetings, but this one would have been one for the ages.

If you don't believe me just open the book to page nine and judge for yourself.

"You can be sitting in your hotel room in the middle of Tokyo and your secretary back home in Arizona can beep you with our newest product. It utilizes satellite technology—the same satellite technology that they used to televise the Olympics. And best of all it only costs $3,500."

While the salesman was talking I was trying hard to imagine (a) why I would be sitting in a hotel room in Tokyo and (b) why my secretary would want to beep me there (your wife wants you to pick up a loaf of bread on the way home). Seeing my lack of enthusiasm for the high tech beeper, the salesman proceeded to take me through his entire line: "this one has three different electronic signals; this one provides for two way voice communication; and this one has a leather carrying case."

Finally, he got down to the basic $39.95 unit. "It runs on two double-A batteries, gives off a sprightly but not piercing beep, fits snugly on your belt, and provides the capability of one way voice communication—your secretary can talk to you but you can't talk to her."

"I'll take it."

Buying a beeper is something I never thought I would do. Beepers had always annoyed me. I first became aware of them about fifteen years ago. In those days very few people had beepers. They were mostly worn by doctors.

One doctor I knew—Dr. Jordan—wore his beeper to Mass every Sunday. He was always on call to deliver babies, and without fail his beeper went off five minutes into Father Fitzhugh's sermons. This was annoying to Father Fitzhugh and to those of us who were trying to sleep.

Gradually I began to notice more and more people wearing beepers not only in church but also in restaurants, movies, theaters, parties, concerts, and even on the tennis court. It got to the point that everywhere you went to get away from the pressures of work you became an unwilling audience to a veritable symphony of beeps, buzzes, and electronic pulses. There is nothing like the sound of an office pager to make your stomach tighten with stress. To me the proliferation of beepers was as threatening to our American lifestyle as the spread of polyester fabrics.

In ten short years, what had once been an elite status symbol of the medical profession had become a tool of the common man. Not only were beepers now in evidence at an array of recreational events and social gatherings, they were also being worn by a wide diversity of people. Everyone carried a beeper—accountants, drug dealers, lawyers, school principals, and even newspaper boys.

In the face of this growing trend, I became more and more determined to make it my single purpose in life not to wear a beeper. To me a beeper looked suspiciously like an electronic leash, and, at the time, I was strongly opposed to putting leashes on human beings. What, I would ask myself, could happen in a library that would be so important that I would need to be contacted immediately.

But all of those feelings changed when my new library was being built and I became a full-time construction manager. On an increasing basis I was out in the field conferring with architects, designers, and contractors. This became a source of frustration for the staff. "It is becoming increasingly obvious to everyone," said a frustrated employee, "that you are becoming more and more inaccessible. There are times when we need to contact you."

I was flattered by this statement, so flattered that I purchased the $39.95 beeper. It took me a while to get used to. At first it felt very foreign, like a retainer in your mouth or a splint on your finger. But after a while it became such a part of me that I actually felt somewhat incomplete when I wasn't wearing it.

What I didn't expect to experience was a growing feeling of dependence on my beeper. For forty years of my life I had gotten along just fine without a beeper but then all of a sudden I couldn't imagine living without it. In that sense it was similar to any other technological gadget like a car phone, lap top computer, word processor, or microwave oven. Have you ever looked back at your life and marveled that you were able to survive your first thirty years without a microwave oven? It doesn't take long to become addicted to new technology.

Beepers are no exception. I came to realize that far from being an electronic leash, a beeper can be an instrument of freedom. While previously I may have been reluctant to spend an extra hour at the construction site for fear that the President of the Board would be back at the library expecting to see me in my office, the beeper allowed me to do just that. If he wanted to see me, my secretary could simply beep me. I developed a great appreciation for my beeper when I understood how it allowed me to be away without being out of touch.

But I also learned that the beeper could do something else for me.

Used properly, it could endow me with a certain image. Let's say you are going before the City Council at budget time and you want to ask for additional administrative support staff. You can do this by (a) throwing reams of statistics at the council that will probably not be fully understood or believed, or by (b) instructing your secretary to beep you at thirty second intervals during your presentation in order to create the illusion that you are being torn in twenty different directions at once. I would suggest that "b" is the more effective strategy.

I also learned that beepers can be used to pull you out of tight situations that you don't want to be in. That meeting on budget cuts with the finance director that you are required to attend can be much less painful if you have your secretary beep you and say "The Mayor is on the phone, and he wants to make it clear that under no circumstances should the library's budget be cut!" In that situation, the beeper's one way communication capability is a Godsend.

Yes, I came to learn that the beeper is like all technological tools. The key is to harness its power in creative ways. Once I even used it to get out of yard work. It was a Saturday afternoon, a beautiful Saturday afternoon, and my wife put a pair of pruning shears in my hands and said, "The pyracantha bushes await." With my trusty beeper it was no problem to get out of that little chore. I simply walked back into the house (under the pretense of having to go to the bathroom), called my best friend back at the library, and told him to beep me in five minutes. "What should I say?" my friend asked.

"I don't know," I said. "Think of some crisis."

So five minutes later while I'm pruning the bushes under the watchful eyes of my wife, the beeper goes off and all of a sudden a voice can be heard saying, "Will, the library is on fire! Get down here immediately!"

This little ploy worked so well that I used it again and again and again. One week the bathrooms were flooded; the next week 300 skinheads were holding a convention in the baby changing room; and the following week someone had hotwired the bookmobile and was headed towards Mexico with it. Suffice it to say that the pyracantha did not get trimmed that month.

And the next week I had a legitimate excuse — the Fiesta Bowl. Six months earlier I had bought a premium ticket to this annual event. "Have fun at the bowl game," my wife said pleasantly as I headed for my car.

"Don't worry, I will," I said. "It should be a great game."

"Be sure and take your beeper," she said. "The way things have been happening at the library on Saturday, you'll need it."

"Don't worry," I said. "I never go anywhere without it."

There I was a half hour later sitting on the fifty yard line and waiting for the opening kickoff when my beeper went off. It was my wife.

"WILL, HURRY HOME! THE HOUSE IS BURNING DOWN!"

I rushed out of the stadium and speeded home with reckless abandon. All I could think of was the welfare of my wife and kids. But when I got home they looked surprisingly calm . . . and the house looked surprisingly normal. There had been no fire.

My wife smiled at me as I got out of the car, and then she handed me the pruning shears. "The pyracantha await," is all she said.

THE $500 TOILET SEAT

Let's say that you're at a dinner party. On one side of you is Wile E. Coyote and on the other side is Roadrunner. What subject matter can you possibly bring up that will not put you right in the middle of an unpleasant argument? I suggest that you start talking about taxes.

There is a great deal of unity about taxes. Everyone hates them. I don't care if you are white, black, rich, poor, well educated, or poorly educated, I'll lay hundred to one odds that you hate taxes. You will, from time to time, find people who claim to support the concept of taxes, but you will never find anyone who actually enjoys paying taxes.

"Do you enjoy paying taxes?" I once asked a library school professor who had just finished giving a two hour lecture on the need for greater tax support for public libraries.

"About as much as I enjoy being gagged, beaten, and robbed," was his answer.

We public librarians are in an uncomfortable spot when it comes to taxes. We like to complain as much as anybody about the sizable chunks of our paycheck that are claimed by everyone from the Chairman of the Joint Chiefs of Staff to the county dogcatcher. But we also know that there is a certain hypocrisy to our whinning that is commonly called "biting the hand that feeds you." The unpleasant truth is that we live off of taxes. They are our livelihood.

To cope with the growing hostility over taxes, we in the public sector have had to learn an entirely new way of talking to our constituents. Rule #1 is to never use the word "tax" or "taxes." Instead we need to use expressions like "revenue enhancement opportunities" or "value added surcharges." I know this because this morning I watched President Bush's press conference on the budget deficit. He used those terms. I wasn't sure what he meant by "revenue enhancement opportunities" or "value added surcharges" until Dan Rather explained that he was talking about taxes—specifically "sin taxes."

A sin tax according to Rather is a tax on products that are sinful to use—things like cigarettes, liquor, and gasoline. I assumed that the gasoline was being taxed because it can be used as an inhalant to get high. Certainly driving a car cannot be considered a sin, can it?

The sin concept is a rather ironic one. The President, if Rather was correct, is apparently depending upon smokers and drinkers to balance the federal budget. That's a heavy responsibility to put on the shoulders of sinful people. One wonders if there won't be a national campaign to "Just Say Yes." One also wonders if there won't be a big push to legalize marijuana, cocaine, and hashish. Our new national motto could be "tune out, turn on, and pay off (the national debt)".

Actually, a better way to go would be to extend our definition of what a sin is. Personally I don't think drinkers and smokers are our only sinners. I have a whole list of sinful products that should get the value added sin surcharge. Polyester pants, yellow neckties, strong perfumes, spandex sweat suits purchased by overweight people, cowboy boots, bolo ties, microwavable pizzas, pinky rings, gold chains, electric shoe polishers, double stuff Oreo cookies, goo-goo clusters, car phones, tickets to mud wrestling matches, and noisy beepers should all be sin taxed.

This concept could also be applied to services, and I'm not just talking about the usual stuff like prostitution, massage therapy, or pornographic phone lines. There are many other disreputable services that most definitely should be considered, if not sinful, at least shady. These include all legal services, breast enhancements, and dog walking services.

Dogwalking is a good example. If you have to hire someone to walk your dog, you deserve to pay a hefty value added surcharge. Personally I think that people who have to pay other people to walk their dogs should not be allowed to own dogs. But then that would put a lot of dogwalkers out of business, which would be bad for the economy. It's much more productive to tax sin than to ban it. You should be allowed, therefore, to hire a dogwalker but only if you're willing to pay the extra tax.

Of course there's another more profitable and more direct approach to creating new revenue opportunities and that is for the government not just to tax the sin but provide it as well. Actually, this is not a new idea. Out state governments have been doing it for years with lotteries. The word "lottery" of course is nothing more than a euphemism for gambling—gambling at very, very bad odds. If Las Vegas casinos offered the kind of odds that state lotteries offer they would go out of business in no time. The only reason that people buy state lottery tickets is because it is the only game in town. They have no other options unless they want to travel to Nevada, Atlantic City, or Deadwood, South Dakota.

Why is it the only game in town? Our state governments have hypocritically determined that gambling is a social evil and have therefore outlawed it. But having declared it a sin, what do those very same governments do? They turn right around and set up their own enormously profitable electronic numbers game and call it a lottery. But the worst part of the hypocrisy is that the states not only run the world's biggest bookie joints, they do so at scandalously bad odds. How can the state get away with setting such bad odds? Simple, they have outlawed all the competition. The bottom line is that our state governments not only provide a sinful service, but they do so in a greedy, sinful manner.

How long will it be before our governments extend their gambling monopolies to other tasteless activities like providing our citizens with narcotics, prostitution, and pornography? The deeper our budget deficits grow, the greater is the possibility that this will happen.

Wouldn't it be refreshing to see governments take a more positive approach to taxes? Wouldn't it be nice to see a politician refer to a tax as a tax and not as a revenue enhancement opportunity? I mean it's not like our taxes are being used to finance the international drug trade or the baby black market. For the most part, taxes are used for good things like defense, food for needy families, highways, schools, and libraries.

What the government needs to do is take a United Way ("thanks to you it works") approach. National Football League players should get on t.v. with inspirational music playing in the background and say "Our government needs your money for cancer research, medical services for the elderly, and libraries for young people." From time to time when I look at my paycheck stub I fantasize that with my taxes I am assisting a needy family or helping to develop a cure for heart disease.

But that is fantasy. The reality is that the good things that taxes do rarely catch anyone's attention. It's the $400 toilet seats and the $200 ashtrays that get all the attention. I know one librarian who pays around $400 in federal tax per pay period. Everytime he gets his paycheck he says, "I've just bought the Air Force another toilet seat." That is a typical attitude. Most people see the government as some great big bureaucratic black hole that sucks up their tax money and gives them nothing back in return, and they see the Internal Revenue Service as an industrious army of coldblooded tax auditors who would like nothing more than to take their home and business abruptly away from them. Is there a less popular institution in the country than the

Internal Revenue Service? Are there three other letters in the alphabet that strike more terror in the hearts of Americans than the letters I.R.S.? I think not. Why then has the library profession decided to link arms with the I.R.S., and why have we consented to become one of the country's biggest distributors of tax forms and tax instruction booklets? The answers lie completely beyond my ability to comprehend.

For seven or eight years now, good hearted, well intentioned librarians have befriended the most unpopular people in the world. Some people say that our servitude to the I.R.S. is admirable. They say that we are providing an important service to library patrons. I say that we are being just plain stupid. It didn't take me more than one April 14th afternoon at the reference desk to form that conclusion. In my short stint at the desk I handled forty-eight complaints, a world's record for a four time period, but not one of those complaints was related to legitimate library business. Every single one dealt with taxes. In fact every single reference question that I handled that afternoon dealt with taxes. In the eyes of the people who came to the library that afternoon, I was not a librarian. I was an employee of the Internal Revenue Service.

As an employee of the I.R.S. I was open game for verbal abuse. Since it was the year of the famous $400 Air Force toilet most of the abuse was of the tacky bathroom variety. "I hope you have fun using your four hundred dollar toilet" and "I'd hate to think of what you must pay for a roll of toilet paper" were two of the kinder remarks that I had to endure that day.

It was by far the longest four hours I have ever spent at the reference desk, and just when I thought that I had heard my last complaint a man approached me five minutes before closing. "I need your help!" he said with an air of urgency.

"What is it?" I asked wearily.

"It's about my ex-wife," he said with some pain.

"I'm sorry," I said, "but I'm really not in the counseling business."

"No, no, it's not that," he said.

"Then what is it?" I asked.

"It's a tax question."

"Are you looking for a particular tax form."

"No, I need advice. Here's the deal. Twenty years ago my wife and I purchased a townhouse. Then four years ago we got divorced. I moved out of the house and she stayed in. We agreed that when our son reached the age of 18 that we would sell the house and divide the equity half and half. That will occur next month. Instead of paying a tax on the capital gains can I roll it over into another house?"

"You're asking me?"

"Yes."

"I'm sorry I can't help you. I'm a librarian, not a tax accountant. I can show you some books on tax law that might help you but I really cannot give you advice."

"WHAT DO YOU MEAN YOU CAN'T GIVE ME ADVICE? YOU WORK FOR THE I.R.S.!"

"No, I work for the library."

"WHAT GOOD ARE YOU? YOU WORK FOR THE I.R.S. AND YOU CAN'T HELP ME.

"WHY CAN'T THEY HIRE SOME SMART PEOPLE!"

"I'm sorry, sir, but I work for the library."

"YEAH, BUT YOU'RE STILL A GOVERNMENT PARASITE!"

"Is that all, sir?"

"NO, I HAVE ONE MORE QUESTION. CAN YOU AT LEAST TELL ME WHERE THE MEN'S ROOM IS? I THINK I'M ABOUT TO BE SICK."

"The men's room is right over there," I said pointing to an area in back of the circulation desk. "I'm sure that you'll like it. We've supplied it with the finest furnishings. Even the toilet seats are the best money can buy. They cost five hundred dollars, a hundred dollars more than what the Air Force spends."

The expletive that he threw back at me is not printable here, but it was quite appropriate for the subject of toilets.

STORY OF MY LIFE

From a bibliographic control standpoint, newspapers and magazines are probably a librarian's biggest challenge. They are not only numerous (there are more than 70,000 different periodicals published each year in this country alone), they are maddeningly haphazard. They change in size, shape, publication schedule, and even title with alarming regularity. In fact, they are anything but periodical in nature. Bringing order and control to periodical collections is like following after a two year old child. It would not surprise me if periodicals' librarians had a significantly higher suicide rate than other types of librarians.

But the efforts of periodical librarians are greatly appreciated. Periodicals provide library users with a deep base of information on an unbelievably diverse range of subject areas. Take your pick. When it comes to periodicals you can get anything from *Sludge* (a fortnightly newsletter devoted to the subject of waste disposal) to the *National Enquirer* (yes, Elvis is alive; yes, a Kansas woman gave birth to a chimpanzee; and yes, Liz Taylor is the product of a sex change operation).

Let's assume that on an average each of the 70,000 periodical titles comes out with a new issue twelve times a year. That totals almost one million periodical issues per year. Of those one million different magazines and journals, which single issue do you suppose gives public librarians the most trouble? No, it's not *Playboy* or *Penthouse* or *Hustler* because you will not find those publications in the overwhelming majority of public libraries.

The most problematic periodical that public librarians have to deal with, surprisingly enough, is the issue of *Sports Illustrated* that comes out in the first week of February. Librarians commonly refer to that infamous publication as simply "the swimsuit issue." In a word, it gives us fits—especially in the last fifteen years.

The irony of this is that for the fifty-one other weeks in the year *Sports Illustrated* is probably one of the least controversial magazines in our collections. I, myself, am a big *S.I.* fan. Over the past thirty-three years it has been my steadiest companion. I started receiving it on September 24, 1957, for my eighth birthday, and ever since then Thursday has been my favorite day of the week because that is the day when *S.I.* arrives in the mailbox. From the very beginning I liked the magazine because it was such a colorful and unabashed celebration of the holy trinity of American sports—baseball, football, and basketball.

And in 1964 just when I was old enough to begin appreciating such things, *Sports Illustrated* began putting out its infamous February swimsuit issue. At the time, however, it was hardly infamous. I remember it more as an unexpected balmy breeze wafting through the chill of a gritty New Jersey winter than as an unpleasant storm of controversy ripping families apart and driving librarians crazy. In fact that first swimsuit issue was downright demure. Its intent seemed to be to put more of a highlight on the Caribbean resort that served as the photographer's backdrop than on the models being photographed. And, furthermore, the swimsuits that the models were wearing wouldn't have made even the most modest librarian blush.

Gradually, however, it seemed that each February the exotic locale where the swimsuit shots were taken became less visible and the swimsuits became more visible. Actually that's not quite right. The girls became more visible and the swimsuits became less visible. Or to put it another way—the swimsuits began getting smaller and smaller and the models (at least in places) began getting larger and larger. The tone of the swimsuit issue was progressively becoming less of a balmy summer breeze and more of a tropical heat wave. By the middle of the 1970's the swimsuit issue had become hot, very hot. Nowhere was that heat felt more than in the public library. "What are we going to do about the swimsuit issue?" has become as unpleasant a topic as "who is going to get the bookdrop?" or "who is going to work the reference desk on Sunday afternoon?"

Basically three areas of concern have arisen—morality, sexism, and theft. On a moral level, parents do not want their fourteen-year-old son anywhere near the swimsuit issue. Not only do they consider it semipornographic but they also feel that it is the responsibility of the librarian to keep it out of the hands of minors. On a feminist level, women feel the issue to be a horrible form of sexploitation by a male oriented magazine. To them it represents a more dangerous form of sexism than that found in *Playboy* because it is done under the guise of respectability. And third, there is a cut, slash, and steal problem. In the average American library the swimsuit issue is either stolen or mutilated within a half hour after being put into the periodicals collection. Placing it on the open shelves is like putting raw meat in a tiger's cage.

We librarians have developed several strategies to deal with this problem. The first is to simply cancel our library's subscription to

Sports Illustrated. This is a simple, effective, and completely incorrect approach. By not getting *S.I.* at all we have taken care of the morality, sexism, and theft problems, but we have also created a censorship problem by cutting off our patrons' access to the fifty-one other issues and we have committed a ridiculous public relations blunder by taking away a library resource that is wildly popular with most of our male patrons.

Our second strategy is to simply do nothing. The idea here is to treat the swimsuit issue as we would treat any other issue by putting it on the open shelves. In less than a half hour the magazine will be mutilated beyond recognition or it will disappear altogether. As it disappears so do all of our problems. All of our problems but one — we can be justifiably accused of censorship by letting a crime take place without trying to prevent it.

This brings us to strategy number three which is to keep the swimsuit issue behind the periodical desk and police its use very carefully by allowing people over the age of eighteen to check it out for fifteen minute intervals only after they have put down their driver's license, their watch, and a twenty dollar bill as a security deposit. But even this strategy is not foolproof. Apparently the swimsuit issue is more important to some people than their driver's license, watch, or money.

A fourth strategy is to keep the issue in the library director's office on a permanent basis. Here the security is impenetrable. I have always favored this option. If the public has a problem with this approach, all the library staff has to do is explain that the director is reviewing the contents of the magazine to determine its appropriateness in a community library. I have discovered that after a week, people tend to forget about the swimsuit issue, and so you are never really pressed into making a decision. Plus you get to enjoy the magazine.

For many, many years, with few exceptions, I favored strategy number four. One year, however, the swimsuit issue was put out on the open shelves by mistake. By the time I realized this mistake it was too late. The magazine was missing from its rightful spot between *Sports Afield* and *Stereo Review.* I pictured it papering the bedroom walls of some lucky adolescent boy. "That's all right," I said to myself, "I'll pick one up at Wilson's Drug Store tonight." Wilson's was the only store in town that sold a variety of magazines.

"Yes, can I help you?" the man behind the counter at Wilson's asked me.

"I need the latest edition of *Sports Illustrated*," I said.

"Oh, you mean the swimsuit issue," the man said chuckling. "That was completely sold out last night."

"Will you be getting more?"

"Sorry, but no. I wish I could get a thousand more. I'd have them sold in a day."

"Why didn't you order more?" I asked with frustration.

"Because last year I only sold fifty," he said shaking his head and adding, "How was I supposed to know they were going to expose Cheryl Tiegs' dimple in this year's issue."

"What?" I asked with great interest.

"Haven't you heard? In this year's issue Cheryl Tiegs is wearing a fishnet swimsuit, and you can see what appears to be a very interesting dimple."

"What dimple?"

"Well, I wouldn't exactly want to be the one to describe it. It's kind of ambiguous actually. A magnifying glass helps."

"Well, hey, don't you at least have a copy of the magazine that I could take a quick look at," I asked desperately.

"Are you kidding? I put my copy in my safe deposit box at the bank."

Driving home I tried not to think of Cheryl Tiegs' dimple but the more I tried the more I thought about it. By the time I got home it had become somewhat of an obsession. I immediately picked up the phone and called my friend, Norb. "Norb, have you seen the swimsuit issue this year?"

"Yeah, I saw it on the rack over at Wilson's last night. Unbelievable, just unbelievable!"

"The dimple, right?"

"Unbelievable, just unbelievable!"

"Do you really need a magnifying glass?"

"It helps."

"Look, Norb, do you mind if I stop over tonight and take a look at it?"

"Oh, I didn't buy it. I never buy magazines off the rack. I just look."

"Bye, Norb."

The next morning as soon as I got to work I called Sarah over at the school library. "What's up?" she asked.

"It's about the *Sports Illustrated* swimsuit issue. Our copy has already been stolen and we need to make a photocopy of it to keep for our files. Is yours available for photocopying?"

"Be honest, Will. You want to look at Cheryl Tiegs in a fishnet, right?"

"Who me? Of course not. We simply need to complete our files. As you know, *Sports Illustrated* is indexed in *Reader's Guide.*"

"Okay, okay," she said, "hold the baloney. Our copy is in one of the administrator's offices. That's where it always goes—you know, for review purposes."

"Just my luck."

"Sorry, Will."

"Sarah, one last thing. Did you see Cheryl Tiegs' dimple? Everyone's talking about it."

"Yes."

"Do you need a magnifying glass?"

"It helps."

"How was it."

"Awesome. I wish I had one there."

"Where?"

"You have to see it!"

This all happened about fifteen years ago, and I have still not seen the famous dimple. I've searched libraries, book shelves, garage sales without any success at all. I've come to the conclusion that that issue ranks right up there with the Gutenberg Bible in its rarity.

The only time I did stumble across a reasonably intact copy of the magazine, the disappointment was overwhelming. Every picture of Cheryl Tiegs had been neatly extracted. I continue to live in frustration.

Story of my life.

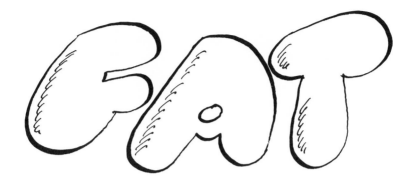

When Robert Burns said that the best laid plans of mice and men often go astray he was probably referring to my educational background.

Twentysome years ago when I sat down at the reference desk as a virgin librarian and awaited the very first reference question of my career, I was brimming with confidence. I felt totally certain that no one could be more prepared for reference and reader's advisory work than me.

As an undergraduate I had studied the classics of Greece and Rome, the literature of the Middle Ages, the poetry of Victorian England, the essays of the New England transcendentalists, the tragedies of Shakespeare, and the comedies of Aristophanes. Then in graduate school I delved into the entire spectrum of children's literature, young adult literature, reference literature, and even genre fiction. I knew books — everything from Dante to Danielle Steele.

So what was my first question, my very first question? A rather rotund woman approached me and asked, "Can you put me on the waiting list for that new watermelon diet book?" That, I am sorry to say, was my professional deflowering, but you know what they say about first times being disappointing. I was optimistic that things would improve and that reference work would prove to be the stimulating activity that everybody said it would be.

Actually I had no idea what this woman was talking about. So I asked one of the women at the circulation desk what the watermelon diet was. She looked at me as if I were culturally deprived. "You really don't know what the watermelon diet is?" she said with genuine shock.

"No, I don't," I said with embarrassment.

"It's only the hottest diet trend of the year," she explained and then muttered something derogatory about librarians with M.L.S. degrees.

I told myself that things would get better. But they didn't. By the end of the day I had gotten five more diet book questions. By the end of the week I had gotten forty. By the end of the month I had stopped counting.

When my library school professors told me that the public library existed to meet the reading and informational needs of the citizenry of our democratic society, I thought they were referring to things like learning how to use a computer, researching the stock market, and studying the issues before an election.

It turns out, however, that the single biggest informational need that people have is how to lose weight. I was not prepared for this because body weight was a subject that I had never really thought much about. To me the world was made up of people who were fat and people who were not fat. I was not fat and I had never been fat. In fact, I had always been trim and athletic. If other people were fat, it was their own fault. For me weight was a moral issue. Fat people ate too much and exercised too little. They had made a conscious decision to be gluttonous and lazy. No one was forcing food down their throat.

Since I considered fatness to be a moral issue, I looked upon the genre of diet books with great disdain. To me they were nothing more than unsubstantiated drivel written by flim-flam artists desirous of making a quick buck. They were not worthy of a library's money or a librarian's time. How could anyone take them seriously? How could reputable publishers produce such tripe?

The more I worked at the reference desk the more the answer became obvious to me. Diet books are very, very popular with fat people and there are a lot of fat people in America. There are more fat people in America than in any other country in the world. In handling diet reference questions I made the startling discovery that there are two types of fat people in America. There are those who are happy being fat and there are those who are not. What really surprised me was that those who are happy being fat are a very small minority of the total population of fat people.

I came to realize that most fat people do not wallow in a kind of Falstaffian delight at being fat. Most fat people want to lose weight. This is where I got confused. If fat people really didn't want to be fat why didn't they just stop eating seven square meals a day. But then after I started looking at the library's diet books I began to realize that fat people didn't want to lose weight by cutting back on their food intake. Fat people literally wanted to have their cake and eat it too, and the diet books told them that they could do just that.

While I would have liked debating the relative merits of Dickens, Thackery, and Fielding with my patrons, I often ended up discussing the pros and cons of the "eat all you want diet," the "candy diet," the "coconut diet," the "grapefruit diet," the "apple pie diet," and of course the "watermelon diet." I considered it completely beneath me and my educational background to give these fad diet books the time of day. So eventually when fat people asked me for a good book on how to lose weight, I got into the practice of handing them a calorie counting handbook and a book on the joys of jogging. This strategy was effective. Eventually fat people stopped coming to me for help. I am now convinced that a major reason why I decided to get into library administration was to avoid the unpleasantness of having fat people ask me for diet books, and once I was safely ensconced in the director's office I could with all the moral outrage that I could muster bemoan the fact that the diet industry was quickly replacing the automotive industry as the quintessential American business. The interest in health, fitness, and diet progressed commensurately with the growth in our fat population, and every quack in America was eager to make a buck on our nation's oversupply of fat people. I would sit back in the sanctity of my office and complain vociferously to my librarians that they were spending far too much of the taxpayers' money on the charlatans who were writing diet books. With horror I watched our diet book collection grow fat with asinine titles like *The James Coco Diet*, *The Endocrine Control Diet*, and *The Delicious Diet*.

"Whether you like it or not, people want these books, Will!" is what one of my reference librarians told me. I noticed with a sense of ironic pleasure, however, that he was a bit on the chubby side.

In response I answered, "Back in my day as a reference librarian when someone asked me for a diet book I would defiantly give them a calorie counter."

A few hours later I overheard my reference librarian telling another staffer that "Manley was probably as popular a reference librarian as he is a director." This snide remark didn't bother me as much as it ordinarily would have when I noticed that the librarian he was speaking to was also on the heavy side. There was obviously a conspiracy of fat people at work in the world.

Several years went by and the diet section of the library had become downright obese. It contained the same old outpouring of con artistry with one subtle difference. The new diet books seemed to have a more geographic taste to their titles. The *Scarsdale Diet*, the *Beverly Hills Diet* and the *I Love New York Diet* were now all the rage, and I continued to sit back and be extremely bitter about so much of our book budget being eaten by the reading appetites of overweight patrons.

Then something horrible happened. I got fat. It all happened very suddenly after my thirty-fifth birthday. From the time I was eighteen I had maintained my weight at a steady 165 pounds, not bad, I always thought, for a guy that was 5′11″. I should have recognized the warning signs: the tightening collar, the derisive remarks from my wife and kids, and the pain of putting on my pants in the morning. But I just didn't think of myself as being fat. I assumed these things were just a function of the holiday season.

The painful truth hit me, however, when someone posted pictures of the staff Christmas party on the bulletin board of the lounge. Among those snapshots was a photo of a fat man giving a toast. Upon closer inspection I realized that the fat man was me.

My instant reaction was to jump on the bathroom scale as soon as I got home that night. Things were much worse that I had dared imagine. The scale said I weighed 202 pounds. I was convinced that the scale was broken, and it turned out that I was right. A more accurate scale that my wife kept in the closet said that I was 204 pounds.

"Why didn't someone say something to me?" I asked my wife and kids at the dinner table.

"Why do you think I started calling you rootbeer belly?" asked my ten-year-old son.

"Well, that settles it," I said. "I am not eating dinner. In fact I am not going to consume anything but sparkling mineral water and watermelon slices until I'm down to 189."

So that night I didn't eat any dinner, or my usual bedtime snack. But that night I woke up at 2 A.M. with hunger pains. I got up, went to the bathroom, and then headed right for the kitchen where in a seven minute timespan I devoured a ham and cheese sandwich, a soft pretzel with mustard, three scoops of chocolate ice cream, a Pepsi, and three handfuls of raisins. After that I had no trouble sleeping.

That day was pretty much a microcosm of the next three years of my life — fast and binge; binge and fast. One month I might weigh 190, the next I'd be up to 205. Finally, I got tired of being fat.

I did what I thought I was never capable of doing. I sneaked into the diet book collection and began rummaging desperately through books with titles like *The Last Chance Diet* and *The Diet Book for People Who Cannot Diet.*

And then I felt a slight tap on my shoulder. It was the reference librarian whom I had berated several years earlier. "Are you looking for this?" he asked with a smile.

In his hands was a book — a skinny, little book entitled "The Calorie Counter."

One of the reasons I've never second guessed getting into the library profession is that it has given me an opportunity to work with a lot of very interesting and very committed library trustees. In the last twenty or so years I've worked with almost two hundred different trustees and was really only disappointed by one of them.

In fairness I should say that the one individual I did not like was also a very committed person. The problem was that her committment was focused on one very narrow issue — getting me fired. The other 199 trustees, however, were absolutely great. They were hard working true believers of the public library cause.

A strong board of trustees is a director's best friend. When the local political wars become stormy and turbulent, library directors are as helpless as the humble jellyfish. I have heard other directors complain about their boards, but I can honestly say that my own boards have always given me a lot more than I ever gave back in terms of good old fashioned common sense, political savvy, and unbending support.

One of the best trustees I ever had was Webb Wilson. When he first came on the library board that I was serving years ago, Webb was retired. No one was ever quite sure what it was that Webb had retired from, but Webb was definitely retired. He was a quiet man who kept to himself. No one seemed to know much about him other than the fact that he had a great love of Shakespeare, Faulkner, and Hemingway. Those were the three things that Webb loved to talk about.

Because Webb was so quiet, there was a lot of scuttlebutt about him. Some people said that he was rich, others said he was just getting by. Some people said that he was divorced, others said that he was a widower. Physically, Webb was an impressive guy. Tall, wiry, and rugged, he reminded me a lot of the Marlboro Man.

The one thing I know for sure about Webb was that he always treated me royally. Webb was a rock of support who brought a finely honed love of books and learning to the board table whenever he was there. That was Webb's one big drawback — a lot of the time he was not there.

You could never really anticipate Webb's comings and goings. For months he would be the perfect trustee — punctual and prepared. And then suddenly and with no forewarning he would be absent for weeks at a time — gone, it was rumored, to some obscure corner of the globe to pursue one of his many adventurous avocations. That was the one positive aspect of Webb's sporadic attendance. It was fun to speculate where this cosmopolitan Marlboro Man had gone to now.

Sometimes I imagined Webb as a kind of later day Papa Hemingway figure who was off running with the bulls in Pamplona, drinking wine in Paris, chasing after elephants in Kenya, and fishing for marlin in the Gulf Stream. At other times I pictured him as a kind of corporate consultant called in at a moment's notice to bail some big company out of a financial abyss.

Just when Webb had become a fixture in my world of imagination, he would pop back into the reality of the board room as suddenly and as unexpectedly as he had left. He was not the type of man, however, who liked to talk about himself and his personal life, and so I never really felt comfortable asking Webb a lot of questions. The most that I could get out of him was that he had unexpectedly been called out of town.

The sporadic nature of Webb's library board involvement continued for a number of years before anyone really got upset about it. He was just not the type of guy that you felt like disagreeing with. A rare blend of rock-solid common sense and personal chivalry, Webb was a difficult man not to like. In fact you very much wanted to like him and to have him like you. If, therefore, from time to time he got "called out of town" that was perfectly understandable. After all, this was an impressive man whom you didn't mind sharing with the rest of the world.

But then Webb's departures became more and more frequent and his absences became lengthier and lengthier. Now when he got called out of town he could be gone for as long as four to six weeks. Eventually, the other trustees began to suggest to me that I check with the borough clerk to see what the rules were with regards to attendance requirements for library trustees. Although everyone liked Webb they were starting to be concerned about how his poor attendance record might look to the public. The board had always prided itself on its service record to the community.

Although this was a legitimate concern, I felt like a traitor going over to visit the borough clerk. Webb had always treated me right. There was no way that I wanted to see him getting booted off the board for poor attendance. It would be a humiliation to Webb as well as bad press for the board.

"The ordinance states quite clearly," said the borough clerk, "that

three consecutive unexcused absences constitute grounds for removal."
This made me feel terrible. Webb had already missed two straight
meetings, and the next one was scheduled for Tuesday night.

Tuesday night arrived and Webb unfortunately was nowhere to be
seen. I could tell that his absence was very conspicuous. As I expected,
the board wanted to know what I had found out from the borough
clerk. The report of my findings initiated a rather lengthy and somewhat unpleasant debate about what to do about Webb. Some of the
board members wanted to let Webb off the hook by excusing his
absences; others wanted to get tough and enforce the rules.

The stalemate was finally broken when trustee John Gordon
showed up late. He appeared shaken. "What's wrong?" he was asked
by several of the trustees.

"I just heard about Webb," he said sadly.

"What about him?"

"He died in Cleveland . . . was run over by a truck . . . was buried
six weeks ago by his relatives."

Everyone was very shocked and very quiet. Suddenly Sylvia Bird
spoke up. "That settles it," she said. "To clear Webb's good name I
move that we excuse Webb's absence here tonight."

This turned out to be something that everyone could agree upon.

Again there was an uncomfortable silence in the board room, and
again Sylvia spoke up. "Furthermore," she said, "I move that we excuse Webb's absence at last month's meeting since he was obviously
dead then too."

Once again the motion carried unanimously.

A PATRON'S GUIDE TO THE LIBRARY

Do hair stylists like to go out and get their hair done? Do chefs enjoy
eating out? Do bartenders like to visit the corner tavern for a cold one?
Do ministers prefer to spend their leisure time listening to a good sermon? Do college professors ever long to play the role of the student?

It's not for me to say because I really don't know. But I do know
that there's no place I'd rather spend my free time than inside a good
library. To me the only thing better than being a librarian is being a
library patron. You're probably very familiar with those guys that hang
around the library from nine in the morning until nine at night? In
twenty-five years I'll definitely be part of that group.

What makes libraries so alluring even to someone like me who
spends all of his working days there? The answer has something to do
with freedom. There is no better place to become invisible than in the
guts of a library. You're out of the way of teachers, parents, spouses,
children, television programmers, and radio broadcasters. As a library
patron you're your own boss. You do what you want to do and read
what you want to read. The possibilities are endless. During one afternoon in the library I can sail around the world, hunt for elephants in
Africa, split the atom, travel to Venus, follow Caesar to war, chase
after whales with Ahab, and listen to the silence with Thoreau. Where
is there a better place to spend free time?

That's the way I feel even when I'm traveling. When you go to
Honolulu the first thing you probably want to do is go to the beach,
right? Not me. As soon as that plane touches down I'm on my way to
Honolulu Public. It's that way with all my trips—libraries first,
scenery second. Everyone knows that as canyons go, the Grand Canyon is the big daddy of them all. But how many of you knew that the
nearby Flagstaff Public Library is one of the best places in the entire
American West to spend time? Sure, the Pacific Ocean is one of our
planet's more impressive bodies of water, and I can understand why
you might want to take a leisurely drive down Highway One to get a
good look at it. But on your way you really ought to make a point of
stopping at the San Juan Capistrano Public Library. It'll make your
trek to the ocean worthwhile.

I have been in libraries all over the country. It's my hobby. No, it's
my passion. I've been in big ones, little ones, old ones, new ones, rich
ones, poor ones, friendly ones, unfriendly ones, pretty ones, and pretty
ugly ones. My twenty years of library-trekking, I think, qualifies me
as an expert library tour guide, and guess what I've found out? I now

know, strictly from a patron's standpoint, what separates the good libraries from the bad ones, and surprise, the determining factor is not money.

In fact the absolute worst library I have ever been in as a patron is one of the richest libraries in the entire country—the Dallas Public Library. I visited D.P.L. shortly after it opened. My library expectation level was never higher. I had heard that Dallas was the library Taj Mahal to beat all others. It was supposed to be a multistoried, state of the art, fully computerized, breathtaking monument to public librarianship. The rumor was that it absolutely reeked with money. The truth was that it did indeed reek with money. It reeked very badly with money. It reeked like onions and garlic.

It reminded me of a suburban Chicago shopping mall where I once bought a raincoat. There, right in the heart of downtown Dallas, was an expensive new library that had all of the warmth and character of J.C. Penney's. Visiting this monstrosity was like going to see the Grand Canyon and discovering that it had been turned into a landfill. Several years later when I was ready to build a new library of my own in Arizona I took my architects to Dallas to show them precisely what not to do.

No, money is not everything when it comes to libraries. There's a modest, little library in Porter, Indiana (population 2,988), that has a solid book collection, a fireplace, and a coffee pot that's always perking. Is this heaven? You bet.

Whenever I hear librarians debating the pros and cons of establishing accreditation standards for public libraries, I always think that such a process would be great, but only if I could be the one to set the standards. That's because I've got this business down to a science. I know exactly what is necessary to create a good library. There are five main ingredients: (1) nooks and crannies, (2) a tranquil ambience, (3) Frost/Hemingway/Steinbeck, (4) sticky, chewy chocolate swirl ice cream with nuts, and (5) passionate librarians.

Crooks and Nannies

All good libraries have nooks and crannies—out of the way places where patrons can hole up with a good book without being seen by everyone who walks through the front door. Privacy is a very rare commodity in today's world. Libraries provide a real service by being secular sanctuaries—places of refuge where patrons can escape the stresses and strains of the everyday rat race. When planning new libraries, librarians should make it a point to design in a whole series of interesting nooks and crannies. In fact when I see statistics about new library buildings I am always disappointed that they never include a number for nooks and crannies per square foot.

Beware that any building designed and built during the 1970s is probably a disaster area from a nooks and crannies standpoint because this was a period of openness in architecture. The result was that we ended up with a whole bunch of buildings without interior walls. The open classroom, the open office, and the open library were the unfortunate biproducts of this era. If you have a 1970s vintage library please petition your city council to turn it into a storage bin for highway salt because that's all it's really good for. Next to the polyester leisure suit, the open library was probably the biggest debacle of the 1970s.

A Ranquil Tambience

I know that ambience is a fancy word that yuppies use to describe restaurants, but I can't think of a better one to describe libraries. "Mood" sounds too personal; "environment" sounds too much like earth day and recycling centers; and "feel" sounds too much like an X-rated movie. So "ambience" is really the word that I'm looking for.

Actually ambience is overrated when it comes to restaurants. At least it is for me. When I go out to eat, I'm looking for a good steak, not a fish pond full of carp next to my table with Zen music playing dissonantly in the background. Restaurants would do a lot better by putting their money into food rather than fish ponds.

But libraries are different. For libraries the proper ambience is everything. Actually what I want to get across is not so much how a library should feel as much as how it should not feel. For one thing, it should not have the ambience of an audiovisual center. Any library, for example, that has a television set in its children's room should be bombed to the ground, and any library that has a television set in its children's room that is used by children to play Pacman should be bombed to the ground with its library director locked inside.

Above all else, a library should be a refuge of sanity—a place where you can escape the annoying buzz of radios, televisions, video-games, and videotapes. It should be a place of quiet where learning, reflection, and meditation can flourish. Other things that libraries should not have are electric pencil sharpeners, plastic and metal furniture, posters of rock stars, background music, public address systems, vending machines, neon signage, and bean bag chairs.

A library should have a unique ambience — one that is distinctly different from schools, bookstores, microchip factories, shopping malls, or video arcades. It should be something a bit old fashioned, dignified, and friendly — like that old tweed coat with the wool patches on the elbows that you wear when the weather gets brisk in October.

Stost/Fremingway/Heinbeck

A library with a weak book collection is like a religion with a weak god. It's not the size of the collection that's important, it's the quality. I can't think of a more criminal use of tax money than to fill a library with flash-in-the-pan bestsellers and junky genre fiction at the expense of more enduring and diversified publications.

I feel so strongly about this principle that I've come up with a quick and foolproof way of judging the quality of a collection. All you have to do is check three authors — Robert Frost, Ernest Hemingway, and John Steinbeck. These are the three great American writers who are very, very popular with both Joe Blow, average guy, and Dr. A. Byron Thistlewood, literary critic. There should be absolutely no reason why every single library in America should not have all the books written by these three authors. Therefore, to determine how good your library collection is all you have to do is divide the total number of Frost/Hemingway/Steinbeck titles in your collection by the total number of Frost/Hemingway/Steinbeck titles currently in print. A library with a percentage under 60 needs to get a new book collection developer, and a library with a percentage under 40 needs to get a new library director.

Chicky, Stewy, Swocolate Chirl Nice Cream with Uts

Patrons are a big part of the fun of going to a library. An interesting, diverse blend of patrons is a must. My theory is that interesting libraries attract interesting people and vanilla ice cream libraries attract vanilla ice cream patrons. Personally I prefer sticky, chewy chocolate swirl ice cream with nuts.

The library is the quintessential democratic institution. It is free and open to everyone: blackwhitebrownyellowredrichpooryoungandold. The first thing I do, therefore, when I walk into a library is check out the clientele. If the place is filled with middle-aged white women reading paperback romances then I know I am in Library Hell.

Stassionate Paff

Contrary to public opinion, librarians are not all old, all female, and all ill-tempered. They come in all shapes, sizes, genders, and temperaments. As a patron I like a librarian who has passion, an individual who is not afraid to tell me with unprofessional candor and subjectivity which new books are good and which ones are bad. I like a librarian who has strong feelings and is not afraid to express them. If there's anything we have too much of in the library field, it's something called professional detachment which never allows you to vent your true opinions. I like a librarian with opinions, although I will admit that sometimes the passionate librarian can be a pain in the neck. But as a great Zen master once said, "where there's pain, there's enlightenment."

For instance, just last week I was at a local academic library to pick up some children's books on the subject of homophones. The books were for my wife, a third grade teacher. She needed them for use in her classroom. After finding my way to the library's curriculum collection, I picked out three books, and took them to the check-out desk. Before checking the books out, however, the circulation librarian quickly leafed through them. Then she looked up and said, "I can't check these books out for you."

"Pardon me?"

"I can't check these books out."

"Why?" I asked. "Are they reference materials?"

"No, they're not reference," she said "THEY'RE SEXIST."

"I don't understand. They're on homophones."

"Look at the illustrations. The girls are dressed in frilly, little dresses and the boys are in pants. The girls are cooks, nurses, and mothers, and the boys are doctors, soldiers, and firemen. The girls are petite and the boys are big. It's one of the worst examples of sexual stereotyping I have ever seen."

"Be that as it may," I said, "I have every right to check these books out and I intend to do so."

"The only way I'll let you have these books is if you promise that you'll burn them."

"Look," I said, "YOU'RE BEING VERY UNPROFESSIONAL. I HAPPEN TO BE A LIBRARIAN AND I KNOW WHAT MY RIGHTS ARE."

"YOU'RE THE ONE WHO IS BEING UNPROFESSIONAL!" she screamed. "AS A LIBRARIAN YOU SHOULD BE TOTALLY OPPOSED TO SEXUAL STEREOTYPING IN CHILDREN'S LITERATURE!"

"I INTEND TO CHECK THESE BOOKS OUT NOW! LET ME HAVE THEM OR I'LL SEE YOUR SUPERVISOR AND MAKE SURE THAT YOU GET FIRED!"

That seemed to get her attention. She lowered her voice and asked, "Okay, I can see that you're so sexist that these books can't make you any worse than you already are. Why, in heaven's name, do you want them anyway?"

"They're for a third grade class that's studying homophones," I said nonchalantly.

"THAT'S DESPICABLE. YOU CAN'T LET KIDS ANYWHERE NEAR THESE THINGS, YOU MALE CHAUVINIST PIG. GO SEE MY SUPERVISOR. I WON'T CHECK THESE BOOKS OUT TO YOU."

"VERY WELL," I said, "I'LL GO SEE YOUR SUPERVISOR." Then I grabbed the three books, marched upstairs to the administrative offices, and demanded to see the circulation librarian's supervisor.

"It will be a minute before she gets off the phone," said the secretary.

While I was sitting and waiting it dawned on me how stupid I felt defending my right to check out what really were three very blatantly sexist books. I felt like a sleazy lawyer defending a guilty rapist. But here I was. I couldn't back out now.

"May I help you?" asked the supervisor. "I understand you have a complaint."

"Yes," I said. "It's about these three books. They are very sexist. The sexual stereotyping in the illustrations is almost scandalous. A fine library like yours should not stoop to this level. Just think, these books might get into the hands of children."

As I was talking, the supervisor paged through the books with great interest. After a long pause, she looked up at me and said, "I am very impressed that someone like yourself — a man even — would be so sensitive about such an issue. Quite frankly I am embarrassed that these books somehow got into the curriculum collection. Thank you very much for bringing them to my attention. It's concerned patrons like you that make librarianship such a satisfying field to work in."

I walked proudly downstairs toward the circulation desk. The circulation librarian was waiting anxiously. "Well, she said, "is she going to let you check out your books?"

"HOW COULD YOU SUGGEST SUCH A THING," I said. "THOSE BOOKS ARE BLATANTLY SEXIST!"

PROGRESS

When you're young and in college and looking for work, especially in the summer, you'll say anything to get a job.

"Have you ever driven a bookmobile?"

"No, but I did spend a summer driving an eighteen wheel truck between Cleveland and Chicago."

The truth is I'd never driven anything larger than a four wheel Ford Falcon. But I needed a job and driving a bookmobile sounded like it would be a greater service to mankind than mopping floors or washing dishes. And it paid more.

The story about the eighteen wheel truck was effective. I got the job. Keeping the job, however, was more difficult, and I'm not just talking about the duration of the summer. I'm talking about the first five minutes. That's how long it took for disaster to strike.

The bookmobile was parked in very tight quarters behind the library loading dock. Never one to put much stock in rear view mirrors, I turned the key, shifted into reverse, and lurched backwards. Almost immediately I heard a crunch – not a long, jarring crunch, just a short simple crunch, the kind that you get when you step on a coke can. Figuring that I had run over a metal trash receptacle, I shifted into park and hopped out. The trash can that I hit turned out to be a '57 Thunderbird convertible.

I had killed it. It didn't take me long to reach that conclusion. The engine getting knocked into the trunk was a pretty good clue. My first reaction was anger. Who would be so stupid to park a precious little sportscar behind a bookmobile in a no parking zone to boot? I decided that whoever owned the car deserved to get it smashed. People think they can park anywhere.

Shaken but not defeated, I headed up to the administrative offices to report the accident to the library secretary. "Some idiot illegally parked his car behind the bookmobile and I totaled it," I said.

The secretary, a petite woman with closely cropped hair and a sharp, pointy nose, looked up at me blankly and asked, "What kind of a car was it exactly?"

"A '57 T-Bird."

"That idiot was the library director," she said sharply.

"Well, he shouldn't have parked there."

"That," she said very impatiently, "is his private parking space."

"Oh," I said very quietly and then added, "what do we do now?"

"If you value your life you will give me the keys to the bookmobile and sign this paper. It is your notice of resignation. I will make it effective immediately."

Like an obedient child, I laid down the keys, signed the form, and hurried out the door.

I would hate to think that this youthful indiscretion has unduly influenced my thinking on the value of bookmobiles, but the truth is I harbor great doubts about the service effectiveness and cost efficiency of owning, operating, and maintaining a bookmobile. To me a bookmobile is nothing but a twenty ton band-aid that library directors use to provide service in areas where there is not enough population, support, or money to build, operate, and staff a permanent library facility. A bookmobile is a very poor substitute for a real library. Wouldn't we be better off creating books by mail programs or even setting up volunteer-run branches? In our era of high energy and automative costs a bookmobile makes no sense at all.

The unfortunate reality is that bookmobiles only spend an hour or two in any one location and no one can ever remember the bookmobile schedule well enough to show up at the right time. Even if you do happen to remember the schedule and you do get to the right place at the right time you won't find anything to read. Usually what you get in the typical bookmobile collection are the rejects from the main building. But the worst problem with bookmobiles from a user's standpoint is the climate. In winter bookmobiles are iceboxes; in summer they are ovens. But that's just my opinion.

Given this opinion how do you think I answered an interview question about bookmobiles at a library where I applied for a job? That's right I lied. Again. The library in question used bookmobiles extensively. "Bookmobiles are great!" I said. "They provide a service-effective and cost-efficient way to reach readers in remote areas."

Naturally I got the job, and two months later I was back behind the wheel of a bookmobile. This time I was supposed to drive it into a new bookmobile station that was being dedicated by the mayor and selectmen in the outlying village where it was located. "We want you there, Will, to drive the bookmobile to the new stop and say a few words on behalf of the library."

So at the appointed hour I drove the bookmobile to the designated location, and I actually did pretty well. I didn't hit any people or any cars. I did, however, in full view of the mayor and selectmen, sideswipe the side of a park ramada (don't ask how I happened to end up in a park). All in all, things could have been worse. The damage to the ramada was less than $500 and the damage to the bookmobile was less than $5,000. In the words of one of the children who were attending the dedication ceremony, the bookmobile was not totaled; it was halved.

Many, many years later and much to my surprise when I took my current job with the public library in Tempe, Arizona, I found a bookmobile parked in back of the building by the loading dock. It was a particularly large bookmobile painted a garish shade of orange. On its bumper were inscribed the words "We Really Move Our Tales For You." This disturbed me greatly. I hadn't had to deal with a bookmobile for over a decade and I wanted to keep it that way. "What's that thing doing there?" I asked one of the librarians.

"We run the bookmobile to eighteen different stops."

"No one told me about it at the interview," I groused.

"Oh, it's really not a big part of our overall program."

"I don't care," I said, "I would have never taken this job if I had known about that bookmobile."

"Why?" the librarian asked.

"Because I am philosophically opposed to bookmobiles."

"What is your philosophical opposition based upon?"

"Past experience," I answered. "Crack-ups. Some people have trouble hitting a golf ball. I happen to have trouble driving a bookmobile."

"Oh well, don't worry. You'll never have to drive it here. We have Millie, Carol, and Colleen. They are all excellent drivers and great with the public too."

"You really don't think that I'll have to drive it?" I asked hopefully.

"Of course not. You're the director, and we've got Millie, Carol, and Colleen."

MillieCarolandColleen—that became my mantra whenever the subject of the bookmobile came up:

"Hey, Will, how's bookmobile circulation?"

"Ask MillieCarolandColleen."

"Will, what are the annual costs of running the bookmobile?"

"Ask MillieCarolandColleen."

"Will, we need someone to drive the bookmobile in the City parade."

"Ask MillieCarolandColleen."

"Will, Sparkle Car Wash is here. They need someone to back out the bookmobile so that they can get around it with their spray rig."

"Ask MillieCarolandColleen."

This time the mantra did not work. Millie, Carol, and Colleen were not in. "How could this happen?" I asked my secretary.

"Stuff happens, Will. Stuff happens."

"Well then, tell the guys from Sparkle to come back next week."

"Will, here's the keys, you back it out."

"I'm busy."

"It will only take a second."

I took the keys and headed for the door. My manhood was at stake. I realized if I didn't back out the bookmobile, word would spread and I would be ridiculed by my staff for life. That's a long time. On the face of it, my task didn't look too bad. I had to turn the key in the ignition, put the thing in reverse, goose the gas pedal, and back thirty-five feet straight out. There were no curves to be negotiated and no turns to be made. There were only three things I could possibly hit — the two concrete pillars holding up the roof of the loading dock or the trash dumpster that was located about forty feet in back of the dock. I was thirty-five feet away from glory . . . or humiliation. I would soon find out what I was made of. My mind wandered back toward high school pep talks. "What kind of men are you?" my coach would ask when we were in the fourth quarter and behind by twenty points.

With one foot on the brake I began to slowly commence my journey. One foot, brake, two feet, brake, three feet, brake, four feet, brake, five feet, brake . . . I was doing fine . . . ten feet, twelve feet, fifteen feet . . . so far so good . . . clear sailing all the way. Then I got cocky and went from thirty feet to thirty-five feet without braking. Crunch. Oh my God. I had heard that crunch before. It was the crunch of a sportscar. My board president drove a sportscar. Had he driven up behind me? I put the bookmobile in park and hopped out. I knew that I should never have tried this. Some people cannot hit a golf ball. I cannot drive a bookmobile. Why did I have to try to be a macho man? But good God I had not hit a sportscar.

I had hit the trash receptacle.

Is that progress or what?

WELCOME TO THE REAL WORLD

I had a storybook childhood growing up in the backyards and play-
grounds of Pitman, New Jersey. There is a common misconception
about New Jersey. Everybody thinks that the whole state looks just
like the city of Cleveland and consists entirely of turnpikes, parking
lots, abandoned factories, junkyards, and toxic waste dumps.

Nothing could be further from this stereotype than Pitman. Pitman is a small borough (population 8,500) nestled comfortably in the
middle of the picturesque South Jersey truck farming country. Whoever named New Jersey the "Garden State" must have lived in Pitman
because everybody there has a vegetable garden in their backyard. It
is the kind of place where people take a great deal of pride in their
tomatoes.

The other important thing that you should know about Pitman is
that its official motto is "Everybody likes Pitman." This is not just
civic posturing, it is absolutely true. Everybody does seem to like Pitman. In fact I never met anyone who didn't like it.

Actually, most people love it. They love its clean air, its friendly
citizens, its neat and tidy front yards, and its pretty little schools and
parks. Pitman is front porch America. It is 4th of July parades, sopho-
more sock hops, Friday night football games, Thanksgiving Day dinners, fires in the fireplace, family picnics, Christmas tree lightings,
and birthday parties. If Pitman were a food it would be tasty and
nutritious peach cobbler that all its restaurants are famous for. Pitman
is a happy and secure harbor in a turbulent world.

In fact, if you were forced to identify one negative thing about Pitman it would have to be that Pitman is so ideal that it does not prepare
you very well for the real world. The neighborhood where I grew up
had its share of eccentrics and bullies. But even the bullies were rather
benign. The worst act of violence that I ever witnessed in Pitman was
Dogdirt Dorman getting lashed with a garden hose by Choo Choo
Coleman, and the worst crime I ever witinessed was when a group of
my classmates stole some wrought iron furniture from a borough councilman's front yard, used it as a prop for the senior prom (the theme
that year was Gone with the Wind), and sold it to the high school prin-
cipal, who was then arrested for receiving stolen property.

Pitman kids (like me) who grow up in Beaver Cleaver families
and who play baseball, football, and basketball all day long are often
not ready to face the rough and tumble world outside our borough's
friendly confines. We do fine on the tree lined campuses of colleges

and universities, but that only lasts for four years. Initiation into the real world can be delayed for only so long. Sooner or later we all have to take the plunge.

The murky waters of Hammond, Indiana, is where I took my plunge shortly after receiving my M.L.S. Just as everyone thinks of New Jersey as a violent urban jungle so too do they picture Indiana as one big friendly family farm out on the prairie. The irony, however, is that Hammond is hardly the family farm; it's more like New Jersey than New Jersey. Squeezed uncomfortably in the industrial vise of Chicago and Gary, Hammond is dirty, industrial, and drab. I always found it difficult to breathe there. It almost seemed like its many factories sucked the oxygen right out of the air. On weekends I would get in my car and drive just far enough south to where I could breathe again. Then I was fine for another week.

What always surprised me about Hammond was that everyone who lived there thought the environmental conditions were pretty normal. When I told people about Pitman's clear skies and clean streets they would look at me like I was talking about another planet. "That odor you smell," said one long time resident, "is something you will acquire a taste for because it is the stink of success, the pollution of prosperity. We love it."

Not only was the air bad in Hammond, but there was just not enough of it to go around. Hammond, I decided, was probably the most crowded place this side of Bombay. People lived everywhere — in basements, garages, dog houses, bus shelters, even culverts. The city was definitely on the cutting edge of social problems. It had a well developed street culture long before homelessness became a national issue. Actually I think you had to be a certain type of person to survive in Hammond. I was only able to stay for fifteen months. But there are people who live there for a lifetime. These people are tough, street-wise, and apparently unaware that there are more congenial places in the world.

And then there were the trains. Think hard. If you were asked to make a dirty, congested, unlivable city even more unlivable, what would you do? Easy — you would imprison the place with a spidery network of railroad tracks and run trains through this network every thirty seconds. That's Hammond. The city is not really that big, but if you want to get from one end of it to another you'd better pack a lunch because you're going to see more trains than they've got in

Grand Central Station. I came early to the realization that if I wanted to get around in Hammond I would have to learn which intersections had crossing gates and which did not. Once I mastered this, all I had to do was develop enough skill and courage to consistently beat the trains to the crossings. The consequence of failure, I realized, could be rather significant.

In the middle of this urban absurdity proudly stood the Hammond Public Library, where I was hired to work in the reference department. The library was the handsomest building in town. Large and stately, it loomed like a rich uncle among the poor broken down and boarded up retail establishments that cluttered the city's business district. At night the library glowed like a lighthouse of hope in the shadowy downtown area, and into its light and warmth gathered many of Hammond's most desperate people. They used the library to pursue a variety of activities. Some enjoyed muttering nonsensically while pretending to read a book, others fell loudly asleep face down in the newspapers, and still others aimlessly guided their broken down shopping carts up and down the aisles of the book stacks as though the library were a supermarket. But whatever they did they always carried their trash bags — the shiny black plastic thirty gallon bags in which they kept their dearest possessions.

These trash bag people formed a kind of constant human backdrop for the library. They were always there, just as much a part of the place as the atlas stand, check-out desk, or paperback racks. Every morning fifteen minutes before opening, they would be lined up at the front entrance like fleas on a screen door. At night they were the last to leave, always dispersing slowly into the darkness with their black plastic bags shining sadly in the light of the lonely street lamp that shone outside the building. After a while they became invisible to me. I knew that they were there but I didn't really see them. They were easier to accept that way.

I preferred, instead, to focus my attention on the livelier patrons who frequented the library. Hammond was filled with many types of characters that I would never have come across in Pitman in a thousand years. Here there was a rich diversity of con artists, flim-flam specialists, stock market tipsters, street corner scholars, armchair explorers, reading room philosophers, and backyard inventors. By far, my favorite type of patron was the backyard inventor. Curious, inquisitive, and eccentric, this was the guy who was always just one step away from making a perpetual motion machine or perfecting a solar collector that would work on cloudy days. That I put any credence at all in the abilities of these undaunted descendants of Rube Goldberg is a good indication that even in the ragtag world of Hammond, Indiana, my library school idealism still burned very brightly. I wanted desperately to be the librarian who would get credit for putting one of these mad mechanics in touch with the secrets of the universe.

However, in my zeal I committed the cardinal sin of reference work—I got too personally involved in my professional work. One man in particular, Nick, caught my fancy. To the jaundiced eye, Nick appeared to be nothing more than an everyday grease monkey. The rumor was that he ran a modest auto repair business, which catered to low level Mafiosi, out of a dilapidated old garage down the street from the library. Supposedly he came to the library three or four times a day simply to use our sizable collection of repair manuals to check up on tune-up specifications, repair procedures, and parts numbers. I knew, however, from talking to him that that simply was not the truth or at least not the whole truth about Nick.

"Nick," I used to self-importantly tell my colleagues, "is not an ordinary grease monkey. He is, in fact, a respectable man of science." And then I would explain to them, as Nick had explained to me, that he was actually very close to perfecting a device that you could attach to your carburetor and quadruple your gas mileage. This, I told everyone, was a man who was going to change the entire course of the twentieth century. Whenever, therefore, Nick needed information or help I was at his beck and call. As with most human interchanges, however, I expected from time to time to get something in return for my service. This was my mistake.

At that time, the car I was driving, which by the way was the first car I had ever owned, was a rapidly aging Rambler Classic. Shortly into my first Hammond winter it began to give me trouble with something that mechanics refer to as "hesitation." Whenever I stepped full force on the gas pedal the car simply would not move for five or six seconds — a failing that can result in a great deal of unpleasantness when you are racing a train to a street crossing.

"Nick," I asked one day, "could you take a look at my car. It's out in the parking lot."

"What's wrong with it?"

"It hesitates."

"Oh," he said thoughtfully. Then I flipped him the keys, and he ambled out the door. Ten minutes later he was back.

"Carburetor's shot," he said definitively. "But that's the least of your worries. Where'd you get that heap anyway?"

"Out of the paper—the car ads."

"What'd you pay?"

"Hundred-fifty."

"Look, the car's a piece of junk. Engine's worn out. But because you've been a good guy, I'll take it off your hands for a hundred. Just let me keep the keys, I'll take care of the paperwork, and your money will be here tomorrow."

"Okay, thanks, Nick. Thanks a lot."

That night I got home late because I had to walk. My wife was not amused when I told her what I had done. "You'll never see that man, the car, or that money again," she predicted.

"Oh yes I will," I insisted. "Nick runs a garage right down the street from the library. I'll get my money."

"No you won't," she said very matter of factly. "No you won't."

"Oh yes I will," I insisted. "Nick is very prosperous. Rumor is that he does work for Mafia types. I'll bet they pay real well."

The word "Mafia" hung in the air between us like a sword. For several minutes there was an uncomfortable silence. "Do you know what you just said?" asked my wife. "Did it ever occur to you why he might want our car. They bury people in old cars like ours. Think about that, Will. Pray tell, did you at least get the title and the license plates changed?"

"No," I said very, very quietly.

"Well then forget about the money," she said. "The money is no longer important. You'll be lucky if you don't end up in jail for homicide. That will do your library career a lot of good, won't it?"

What my wife said made absolutely no sense to me until the next morning when I ambled into the garage down the street from the library. "Nick around?" I asked a guy who was changing a tire.

"Nobody named Nick works here."

"He's the owner," I said.

"No, buddy, I'm the owner. And my name ain't Nick."

"Well let me describe the guy," I said nervously. "He's got dark hair, he's in his thirties, and he always wears a Cubs hat."

"Don't know him."

"YOU'VE GOT TO KNOW HIM!" I said desperately.

"Look, buddy, I got work to do."

As soon as I got to the library I began to ask everyone about Nick. No one really knew anything about him. Everything was strictly rumor.

My wife, as usual, was absolutely right. Nick never came back, my car never came back, and I never got the money. Now twenty years later I sometimes think that I have spotted the car in a parking lot or junkyard, but it's always a different car. Actually I hope I never find it.

But I'll tell you something. If you want to know where Jimmy Hoffa is I have an idea. My car disappeared about the same time he did.

When I went to school there were smart kids and stupid kids. There were also average kids. It was all right to be smart, stupid, or average. Nobody made a big deal about it because nobody went around labeling kids as "smart," "stupid," or "average."

But now according to the educational gurus who routinely divide up the world according to their own privileged view of reality, there are only two types of kids — "gifted" and "nongifted." The unfortunate thing is that whereas in the old days children were not formally diagnosed, labeled, and pinned down like so many species of butterflies, today there is a strict educational caste system.

As in any caste system, there is a lot of interest in upward mobility. Naturally, everyone would like to be considered gifted. The problem is that very few are. The result of not being a part of that privileged few is low self esteem, inferior educational opportunities, and a lack of societal respect.

All of the unpleasantness connected with this kind of typecasting is exacerbated by the fact that it is being done earlier and earlier in the lives of our children. This, of course, is in keeping with the modern educational thinking that claims that children are shaped irrevocably in the first few years of their lives. Gifted testing, therefore, is being done earlier and earlier. Fifteen years ago it was routinely done in the eighth grade. Next it was done in the fourth grade, and now there are school districts where gifted testing takes place in the first grade. Fifteen years from now I fully expect that the testing will take place a few minutes after childbirth. Look for hospital nurseries to be divided into gifted and nongifted wings. The gifted wing, of course, will be endowed with classical music, educational toys, and mobiles depicting the solar system. The nongifted kids will have to make do with Bart Simpson dolls.

Fortunately our current brave new world has not progressed to that level yet. Obviously such social engineering takes its toll on the psyches of our children, but its effect is even more devastating to the parents. First of all, the average proud parent is not ready to accept the possibility that his or her child is not gifted until the kid ends up in the state penitentiary. Even a disastrous academic record is unconvincing because to the parent such a record does not indicate that Johnny is nongifted, it indicates that Johnny is misunderstood, improperly handled, and or poorly motivated. In fact I have heard parents argue that their child's poor report card is absolute proof that their child is gifted. "Gifted children often get poor grades because they are bored with the busy work that teachers routinely give their students" is their unconventional wisdom. They are also quick to add that Einstein and Hemingway were poor students who did not graduate from college.

Rightly or wrongly, our offspring, more than anything else, reflect who we are. If the child is gifted, we assume that the parents must be gifted. If the child is not gifted we assume that the parents must not be gifted. No parent, therefore, wants to be told that his or her child is not gifted.

What makes everything rather comical is the fact that the intelligence level of most young children is not all that obvious. The slightest verbalization can connote great differences in meaning to two different people. It all depends on your perspective. Parents, for example, consistently interpret everything that their kids do as a sign of greatness. Nothing that their child does is routine or average. In my opinion, therefore, what we should do is simply declare every preschool child in the country as gifted. That would avoid all the problems of typecasting both the children and the parents.

Unfortunately there is a type of parent — the yuppie parent — who is simply incapable of accepting this simple solution. Yuppie parents want their children to stand above the crowd. By definition, yuppies are upwardly mobile. They want the best of everything — jobs, houses, cars, wines, ice cream bars, shoes, and children. And they want their children to have the best of everything. You can always pick out yuppie children by the designer labels on their clothes — the Guess jeans, the alligator shirts, and the cute little L.A. Gear hightops. Normal parents do not spend a lot of money on clothes for kids. The frozen yogurt is also a dead giveaway. Normal parents get their kids a popsicle off the Good Humor truck. Yuppie parents insist on something more trendy.

They apparently think that because their children have been exposed only to the finest things in life that makes them gifted. I first ran into this logic some years ago when a yuppie mother suggested that their two year old son, Brandon, should be placed in our four year old story hour because he was gifted.

"Why do you think he's gifted?" I asked skeptically.

"Because Brandon has been given opportunities that most other two year olds have not had."

"Like what?"

"He goes regularly with us to the opera, he accompanied us to Paris last summer, and he loves to play with my husband's architectural drafting instruments."

"Has he designed any interesting buildings?" I asked with a chuckle.

"Nothing architecturally coherent, but he has created a diverse array of very interesting abstract designs."

"You mean scribbles," I said.

"Not scribbles," she said ardently. "I prefer to think of them as abstractions—bold and inventive abstractions."

"Beyond these bold abstractions what other evidence do you have that would indicate that Brandon is gifted?"

"At four months he began to use his fingers as separate entities from his hands to explore the exterior world. Most children don't do this until six months."

"Anything else?" I asked.

Yes," she said, "his first word was polysyllabic."

"Look, Ms. Kimble," I said, "how naive do you think I am? I may be willing to believe that Brandon has unusual dexterity in his fingers and I may believe that his art work is bold and inventive, but I draw the line at 'polysyllabic.' There's no way that I am willing to believe that the first word out of his mouth was 'polysyllabic.' I mean I didn't even know what that word meant until a few months ago."

"No," replied Ms. Kimball, "you have misunderstood me. He did not say the word 'polysyllabic.' His first word was 'Mommy.' That is a polysyllabic word. It is two syllables. I don't expect him to articulate a word like 'polysyllabic' for at least another year. Mr. Manley, I want my child in that four year old story hour! I simply will not stand by and watch him wilt with children that are intellectually inferior to him!"

"Well, Ms. Kimball, I really think that you're pushing this thing a bit too far. Why don't we just start Brandon out in the two year old group and see how he does."

"Mr. Manley, do I have to pursue this matter above your head?"

"No," I said wearily, "you can put Brandon in the four year old group."

As it turned out little Brandon may have had superior physical and verbal skills, but unfortunately those physical skills did not include being toilet trained. The first time that he had an accident in our story hour room I had to explain to Mrs. Kimball that children who were not potty trained were prohibited, by library policy, from participating in our preschool programs.

She accused me of being anal retentive. In response to that I said, "Ms. Kimball, I'm not gifted; I don't really know what that term means."

"It means that you're overly concerned with enforcing arbitrary and bureaucratic rules and regulations," she said.

"Fine," I said, "but rules are rules and my job is to deal with rules. Our children's librarians are not nursemaids."

"Do I have to pursue this matter with the Board of Trustees?"

"Yes, Ms. Kimball, you do. But good luck trying to explain to the board why your gifted kid is not yet toilet trained."

That was the last I saw of Ms. Kimball. But I did hear of her again at a late night bull session during a state library conference. I was trading war stories with the library director from a neighboring city. "You'll never believe this," he said, "but I had this obnoxious woman insist that her two year old son belonged in the five year old story hour because he was gifted. Have you ever heard of anything so ridiculous?"

"Actually I have," I said. "The kid wasn't even potty trained was he?"

"That's right," he said, "it took us exactly one week to find that out. But, Will, how did you know?"

"Because that gifted kid stunk up my library before he stunk up yours!"

Every time a United States senator or representative gets into a compromising position with regards to sexual, ethical, or moral conduct, I grimace. Sure, it hurts to think that we the people have once again been embarrassed by our elected officials, but that's only part of the pain.

The real hurt for me rests in the fact that everytime I open a newspaper and read about a Congressional scandal it makes me automatically remember the most embarrassing day of my life. To put this into perspective, I have had many embarrassing moments. I have run the wrong way on a football field in front of 5,000 people. I have shot at the wrong basket on a basketball court in front of 3,000 people. I have gotten lost in the woods during a cross country meet. I have driven the wrong way on an interstate highway. I have gotten on the wrong airplane and landed in Columbus, Ohio, instead of Columbia, Missouri. And I have opened a keynote speech to the West Virginia Library Association by saying how happy I was to be in Virginia.

But the humiliation caused by those fiascos pales in comparison to the embarrassment I experienced one morning at the reference desk many years ago. The library was filled with people, and there were patrons lined up at my desk waiting impatiently for help. I was alone. My reference partner had called in sick. Amid all this hustle and bustle, the phone rang. It was an elderly lady. She must have been hard of hearing because she communicated by shouting.

"Hello, this is the reference desk," I said very professionally.

"HELLO IS THIS THE LIBRARY?"

"Yes, this is the library."

"IS THIS WHERE I CAN CALL FOR INFORMATION?"

"Yes, information is our business."

"GOOD. I HAVE A QUESTION?"

"What's your question?"

"WELL, I HAVE THIS NEWSPAPER HERE AND IT SAYS THAT A UNITED STATES CONGRESSMAN WAS ARRESTED LAST NIGHT IN A PUBLIC BATHROOM IN WASHINGTON, D.C., FOR PERFORMING AN ACT OF SODOMY."

"Yes," I said nervously. I wasn't sure but I thought I saw a city councilman entering the library.

"WELL, I HAVE A QUESTION ABOUT THIS."

"What's your question?" I asked. The councilman (he was a Presbyterian minister) was headed my way.

"I WANT TO KNOW WHAT HE DID."

In a very quiet voice I said, "From what you read in the newspaper it sounds like he performed an act of sodomy."

"WHAT? I CAN'T HEAR YOU?"

In a louder voice I repeated what I had said before. When I reiterated the word "sodomy" everyone who had been milling around the reference desk, including the councilman, looked up at me like I was a pervert.

"I STILL CAN'T HEAR YOU!"

I raised my voice again. "It sounds like from the article that he performed an act of sodomy." This time everyone in the entire reference room looked up at me with great disgust.

"I KNOW THAT!" she said. "BUT WHAT EXACTLY IS SODOMY? WHAT DID HE REALLY DO? HOW WAS THIS CONGRESSMAN MISBEHAVING?"

I was now horrified. Given the age and the apparent sincerity of the woman on the phone I had to assume that she was not playing a practical joke on me. She truly wanted the information that she had requested. But how could I possibly begin a dialog with her on the subject of sodomy with all of these people at my desk, not to mention the councilman, who was now looking at me in a most uncomplimentary way.

"Look," I finally said, "I'm very busy right now. There are people lined up at my desk waiting to be helped. I'll be happy to call you back with the information when things quiet down a little around here."

"IT IS NOT FAIR TO MAKE ME WAIT! ALL YOU HAVE TO DO IS LOOK UP THE WORD "SODOMY" IN YOUR BIG DICTIONARY! DO I HAVE TO CALL YOUR BOARD PRESIDENT!"

"No," I quickly said, "you definitely do not need to call up my board president to discuss this subject. Hold on a second and I'll get the big dictionary."

So I walked over to the dictionary stand to see what Mr. Philip Babcock Gove, Ph.D and editor in chief of *Webster's Third International Dictionary*, had to say on the subject of sodomy. I must say that Mr. Philip Babcock Gove, Ph.D., surprised me. The fact is he gave me quite an education on the subject at hand. According to him, the word "sodomy" is a kind of umbrella term that refers to a wide diversity of very difficult and very disgusting activities. No, Mr. Philip Babcock Gove, Ph.D., would simply not do. He was far too detailed and direct for my tastes and the tastes, I had to assume, of my elderly phone caller.

Next to *Webster's Third* proudly stood the *Random House Dictionary*. It too proved to be too short, simple and direct. What had happened to modesty and subtlety? Where could you go to find a nice, mild euphemism when you really needed one?

I decided that if any dictionary were to be more discreet it would be the *American Heritage Dictionary*. After all *American Heritage* is the patriotic chronicler of our nation's proud past—the champion of Pilgrims' pride and the American work ethic. No such luck. *American Heritage* was just as overly explanatory as the others. Thank God they didn't illustrate the definition with a picture.

My next instinct was to try the *World Book Dictionary*. This, the preferred dictionary of nine out of ten elementary school librarians, would certainly display some modesty. Wrong again. It gave the kind of definition that leaves nothing to the imagination.

With a sense of panic I rushed back to the reference workroom where we stored the long out of print *Webster's Second Edition*—old Noah Webster's stolid but reliable bulwark of linguistic information. It was tattered and torn, but at times it came in handy. I hoped that this would be one of those times. Unfortunately, I was still disappointed. Although somewhat more discreet than the others, Noah still took things a little too far.

There was now only one alternative left—the massive twenty volume *Oxford English Dictionary*, the masterpiece next to which all other dictionaries are reduced to insignificance. Here in this dense jungle of words I found just what I wanted—a nice, polite inoffensive definition.

I picked up the phone. "I'm sorry I took so long, madam," I said, "but there seems to be great disagreement among our foremost lexicographers as to the exact meaning of that particular word. It apparently has been used to describe a diverse array of human activities. I decided, therefore, to go to the pinnacle of lexicographic excellence— the *Oxford English Dictionary*. According to the *O.E.D.*, sodomy is an unnatural form of sex."

Again everyone looked up at me with revulsion. I felt like looking back at everyone and saying, "I AM JUST ANSWERING A REFERENCE QUESTION! I AM REALLY NOT A SEX MANIAC!" But instead I kept my cool and waited for my caller's response.

"I CAN'T HEAR YOU! SPEAK LOUDER!" she urged once again.

So I spoke a little louder. "According to the Oxford English Dictionary sodomy is an unnatural sex act." Again about fifty pairs of eyes were riveted upon me.

Then there was this silence as the old woman mulled over what I had said. Finally she spoke: "WELL, I KNOW THAT MUCH. I WANT TO KNOW WHAT EXACTLY THAT UNNATURAL ACT WAS!"

Now it was crisis time. Desperately, I started rummaging through the many dictionaries that I had piled on top of my desk in a futile attempt to wall off the stares of my reference patrons. What could I tell this old lady without humiliating myself even more? What was the next least offensive definition of the word? What was the lesser of the five evils? Finally, I picked up the phone and very defiantly said in a loud voice for everyone to hear once and for all — "SODOMY IS AN UNNATURAL SEX ACT BETWEEN AN ANIMAL AND A MAN!"

The woman at the other end of the line paused, caught her breath, and mumbled "Oh." Then she hung up.

Everyone in the room including the councilman just shook their head at me as though I was completely beyond hope.

Myself, I was just glad that this particular "reference interview" was over. With some satisfaction I put a mark under the category "Reference Questions Answered Correctly" on my talley sheet.

But then a few hours later during my coffee break I got to feeling a little guilty about creating a false impression in that old lady's mind about what that Congressman had done.

What animal do you suppose she thought he had in that bathroom with him?"

Let's say you're looking for a job as a library director, and each month you faithfully look through the position listings in the various professional journals in search of the perfect opportunity. You want a safe and peaceful community with a good school system for your three children; you want a library that has a sound financial base and a supportive board of trustees; and you want a salary that will not qualify you for food stamps.

Each month you see an ample supply of directorships but none of them are exactly what you are looking for. They are either in the middle of an urban war zone or out on the remote fringes of organized society. If by chance the location is acceptable the salary is not. Or if the location and the salary are acceptable the board of trustees has a reputation for going through library directors like Liz Taylor goes through husbands.

You want to be a library director, but you don't want it that bad. So you wait until next month. But next month you are again disappointed. The same old jobs, the ones that nobody else wants, are the only ones listed. It seems as though the plum directorships never open up.

And then one month, when you've practically given up all hope, you read about a job in a nice, safe community out in the gently rolling hills of the upper Midwest — God's country according to the beer ads. It's one of those places where everyone knows the mayor by his first name. Friendly, bucolic, and down home — this is front porch America. And what's even better is that this community has a reputation for having an excellent school system. The phrase "clean country air" is what keeps running through your mind. This is the job that you've always wanted.

Since three hundred other librarians are probably going to be applying for this job, you understand the importance of writing a sterling letter of application. You must make yourself stand out from the crowd. You inventory your talents — you know nothing about computers and very little about administration. You also know very little about public relations but if there's anything you're good at it is talking yourself out of trouble, which is a pretty good definition of public relations. So in your letter you make reference to the fact that you are generally known as a "public relations expert." No that's not quite right. That's not exactly the image you want to get across. It doesn't pack the intended punch. You change it to "public relations genius." Yeah, that's the ticket — public relations genius.

You put the letter, along with your résumé into the mail, and say your prayers every night. A month later they call you for an interview. They're even willing to pay your travel expenses. You figure that they must be in desperate need of a public relations genius.

When you arrive it is love at first sight. This town is exactly what you've been looking for all your life. The people are friendly, the houses are neat and clean, the streets are uncongested, and the surrounding countryside is dotted with picturesque little farms where cows and horses graze contentedly. Just think—horses only a quarter of a mile outside of town. You've never been within 600 feet of a real horse, but you picture yourself taking riding lessons and becoming a member of the local horsey set.

But first things first. There is still the little matter of the job interview to be taken care of. Although you think it goes well, a month goes by and you do not hear anything and then finally you get a letter. Bad news. The letter says that the decision got down to you and someone else—a man with twenty years of administrative experience. You try to picture this man in your mind's eye and conclude bitterly that he's probably not the kind of guy who aspires to be a horseman. He's probably a computer techie. It's their loss; they could have had a public relations genius.

A month later, just when you have finally driven all your fantasies about owning a farm and raising horses out of your mind, you get another letter from the board. It seems that they are in a bit of a pickle. The man to whom they offered the job lasted only two days. He choked on a piece of pork and died. They would like you to come on board.

Your sense of good fortune is tempered by your feelings of sorrow for the deceased. Information that you get later reveals that he was dining at home alone and that his body was not found for a full week. In fact, when he was discovered, one of his hands was still clutching a glass of Arrowhead sparkling mineral water.

You get to the library and find that you have to prove yourself. Everybody knows that you were the board's second choice, and everyone knows that you owe your job to a bit of gristle. You feel like your very presence here is resented and that you should apologize for the other guy's death. You even feel like saying to everybody that you're not the one who gave him the pork. You are not a murderer. You were a thousand miles away when it happened.

But worst of all, everyone knows that you have portrayed yourself

as a public relations genius. Now you must deliver. So you throw
yourself into the new job with great vigor. You persuade the board to
rewrite the book selection policy, revise the circulation policy, expand Sunday hours, and increase the book budget. You put out creative flyers, brochures, and reports. You start a weekly newspaper col-
umn. You get out into the community and make speeches. You do
everything you can to increase library business short of giving away
free lottery tickets.

But after six months, things have really not changed very much.
The board is getting restless ("we thought you were supposed to have
a flair for p.r.") and the staff remains skeptical ("we liked the guy who
died better than you").

You need to make an impact. The summer reading program is
only three months away. This is your big opportunity. If you can fill
the library with children and parents this summer, circulation will
undoubtedly skyrocket. How can this be done? That is the question
that you ask yourself when you wake up in the morning and when you
go to sleep at night. You think about it all the time — in your car, at
your desk, and in the shower. In fact, you've been spending a lot of
time in the shower ever since you saw that psychologist on *Donahue*
say that is where the average person does his most creative thinking.
But the only thing that you have to show for it is wrinkled skin.

One day, out of the blue, a man you do not know calls. He sounds
desperate. He's a farmer. One of his mares has given birth to a colt. He
wants to give it away. Do you know of anyone in the community who
would like a colt. No, you don't know of anyone to give the horse to.

That night, in the middle of your forty-five minute shower —
voilà — you get an idea. You realize that there is an obvious connection
between a pony and the summer reading program. A very popular
genre in children's literature is the horse story. Misty, Flicka, Black
Beauty, Blaze, the Black Stallion, and Smoky have been friends of
young readers for decades. So why can't this coming summer be the
summer of the horse? All the summer reading materials — book lists,
book markers, and buttons — will be designed with a horse motif, and
at the end of the summer the library will raffle off a pony to some lucky
young reader. The "Great Pony Giveaway" is obviously the idea of a
public relations genius.

First thing in the morning, you call the farmer up. "Is that pony
still available?"

"You mean the colt?"

"Colt—pony—what's the difference?"

"There's a difference," he says. "A colt grows into a horse whereas a pony is more of a miniature horse, but yeah it's still available."

"Great, how would you like to give it away as the dramatic culmination to the summer reading program?"

"Will I get my picture in the paper?"

"By all means."

"Then, yes, I will do it."

"Great, just bring the pony down to the library in six months during the last week of August."

Immediately you and your staff start planning "The Great Pony Giveaway" which sounds a lot better than "The Great Colt Giveaway." The summer reading program starts in three months and the production of posters, flyers, bookmarks, booklists, and bibliographies of horse stories begins in earnest. You call the local radio station and newspaper and distribute flyers in all of the elementary schools. You sense that you are about to have a big hit when, in the middle of May, children begin asking, "When can we sign up for the summer reading program?"

On the first day of the program the registration line is so long that it goes out the front door and halfway around the block. In the first week 2,000 kids sign up. You didn'tknow that there were that many kids in the entire community. Last summer's registration was only 434. But this is the summer of The Great Pony Giveaway and you are a public relations genius.

Every day in June, July, and August is a busy one. To qualify for the pony raffle a child must read twenty books. This has a huge impact on circulation. In June it doubles and in July and August it increases by 300 percent.

And then the big day comes—August 29. The President of the Board reaches into the fishbowl to pick out the winner. The crowd is so big that the raffle has to be held in the city park adjacent to the library. A girl named Nancy wins the pony. As she squeals with delight the farmer hands the reins over to her father. He seems both elated and befuddled but has the presence of mind to thank you, the mayor and the farmer. He says, "This is wonderful. We have never won anything before in our life."

The crowd disperses quickly and you head back to your office to pick up your briefcase so that you can head home. "Nice job!" someone says to you. "It's been a great summer." You feel very proud. You're starting to win over the staff.

That feeling of pride changes to amazement, however, when you get out to the parking lot and see the strangest thing you have ever seen in your life. Nancy's father is trying to put the pony into the back seat of a Ford Fairlane. The car is a four door, but still this is ridiculous. First he tries to push the pony in frontwards, and when that doesn't work, he tries to push him in backwards like the horse is going to sit in the backseat and cross his legs.

Sensing an impending disaster you try to slip quietly into your car and drive away, but Nancy's father sees you and calls you over. "Now what am I supposed to do?" he asks.

"Where do you live?"

"In town on First Street."

"Do you have a good sized back yard?"

"No, it's a patio home."

"Do you have any place to put the pony."

"Hey, isn't this a little big for a pony?"

"It's really a colt."

"Which means it will be a horse."

"Right."

"I was going to put it in the carport."

"Good luck."

"Do you have any other ideas?"

"There's a stable — Green Gables — outside of town where you can keep the horse. Their rates are reasonable."

"How much?"

"Fifty dollars a month."

"FIFTY DOLLARS! MY OWN RENT IS ONLY TWO-FIFTY"

"I'm sorry, but look at the bright side. Very few people can say that they own a horse."

"Now that's a really intelligent statement. You're a real genius, aren't you," he says sarcastically.

"As a matter of fact, I am."

I am a Roman Catholic — always have been; always will be. That is the way it is with many people my age who grew up in the Catholic Church before the advent of the reforms of the Vatican Council of 1962.

The Church that we experienced at that time was far different from the one we know today. Cloaked in the mystique of incense, holy water, the Latin Mass, and the Gregorian Chant, the Catholic Church was high religious theater. It made an indelible impression on a young person's mind.

No Catholic, even the most apostatic, can ever forget going to stations of the cross, benediction, High Mass, or confession. Especially confession. Confession was my favorite part of being a Catholic. It still is, although today it is euphemistically referred to as the sacrament of reconciliation. But no matter what they call it, it will always remain "confession" for me and millions of other Catholics.

The theory behind confession is that we are all sinners. But if we confess our sins honestly and contritely to a priest and do the penitential acts that he prescribes, our sins will be forgiven. This kind of a deal is very handy for fallible guys like me who are always saying things we shouldn't say and doing things we shouldn't do. Confession is a kind of divine eraser that wipes our record clean and allows us to start out anew. I don't know what I'd do without it.

For instance, words cannot express the joy with which I received the blessing "Your sins are forgiven" the time I confessed stealing three dollars out of my mother's wallet for the purpose of buying baseball cards. To make things even more joyful, Father O'Malley never mentioned anything about returning the cards or the money, which is the spiritual equivalent of having your cake and eating it too.

But even that joy paled in comparison to the overwhelming relief I felt upon confessing a very grave sin of sacrilege that I had committed as an altar boy. In response to a double dare from Eddie Crawford, I took a swig of altar wine in the sacristy before Mass while Father O'Malley had his back turned. As soon as I tasted the bitter wine I knew that what I had done was a huge, cosmic mistake.

I was fooling around with powerfully spiritual things, and I felt instinctively that the stakes were much higher than they had been when I took money out of my mother's purse. I had desecrated the very blood of Christ!

This misdeed was perpetrated exactly at 7:00 on a Thursday morning. Confessions would not be heard until 7:00 on Saturday night. I was horrified because I knew that what I had done was so egregiously wrong that if I died unconfessed before Saturday night that I would face probable damnation. As my catechism teacher had taught, damnation is not like a temporary jail sentence, it is for eternity. That, I realized, was a long, long time. In a panic I considered asking Father O'Malley for an immediate special confession. However, I was too afraid of him to do this. Father had a terrible temper. I feared his wrath more than God's. I decided to take my chances and wait until Saturday night. Fortunately I didn't die in the interim.

But even that occasion took a back seat to the relief I felt at confessing the time I secretly skipped Mass to play baseball with my non-Catholic friends. This sin was very serious because nothing in the Catholic religion is more important than going to Mass every Sunday. The nature of this offense was heightened because it was not done impulsively on a whim or a dare. It was very carefully and very cold-bloodedly planned and premeditated. But miraculously, through confession, I was able to have that black mark removed completely from my soul.

All of these memories flooded back to me when my son Michael was preparing for his first confession. "What's it like, Dad?" he asked with a great deal of curiosity.

"It's wonderful," I said. "It's like spilling something on an expensive shirt and then putting stain remover on it an actually getting the whole stain out."

"Is that all there is to it?" he asked. "You just go into that closet and tell Father your sins?"

"Well, you have to do your penance," I said. "Father will tell you what to do to earn forgiveness. That's what penance is — a kind of payment."

"Like a library fine, Dad?"

"Yeah, something like that only with prayers instead of money."

"By the way, Dad. You have five overdue books — two months overdue. You left them on the backseat of the car. That's really bad — especially because you're the library director. You ought to confess that."

"No, Michael," I laughed, "God doesn't care about overdue library books. He's got more important things to concern Himself with."

A few days later, Michael and I were sitting in a very crowded Church together waiting for old Father Francis to finish his sermon on divine reconciliation. It was first confession night for Michael and his classmates. Father Francis had a tendency to ramble on. I leaned over to Michael and whispered, "As soon as Father finishes his sermon jump into the front of the line for the confessional. Otherwise we'll be here all night."

Michael responded superbly. As soon as Father finished his sermon, gave his blessing, and headed for the confessional box, Michael jumped into line like a skittish little bullfrog. Then he grabbed my sleeve and maneuvered me in front of him. "You go first," he whispered nervously.

I could understand his fears. Confession, although an occasion for mercy, is premised on a rather uncomfortable notion—you go into a darkened closet and tell your deepest, most shameful secrets to a total stranger. I have been going to confession for thirty years and there is still only one other thing in life as unsettling for me as the confessional box and that is the dentist's chair.

Much of the discomfort obviously stems from the fact that confession is about death. We seek forgiveness of sins so that we might be spiritually cleansed and prepared to meet our Maker when our number is called. Death, even in the context of spiritual resurrection, is not the most pleasant subject around. To a ten year old it can be downright frightening. Michael, therefore, felt it necessary that I go first as if this were some horrifying amusement park ride. If I could survive it, he could too.

There were two people in line ahead of me. One was a matronly old woman who was double clutching her rosary beads and the other was a nun dressed in full habit. You don't see that much anymore. The combined ages of these two women was probably upwards of 160 years—plenty of time to commit a diverse array of mortal sins. I doubted, however, if these two women had done so much as pull a dog's tail in the last fifty years. They were in and out of the confessional in less than a minute. Obviously this was their 95,000 mile check-up and everything was just fine under the hood.

And then it was my turn. Actually I had been dreading this moment. During Father's sermon it dawned on me that I hadn't been to confession for over three years. I had a million excuses—job pressures, writing deadlines, speaking engagements, family responsibilities, and

Monday night football—but I knew deep down inside that the real reason I hadn't gone was simple avoidance. It is human nature to want to avoid at all costs facing up to your personal weaknesses. I had avoided confession for the same reason that fat people avoid mirrors.

But now my hour had come. I approached the confessional as though it really were a frightening amusement park ride—very much like that rocket they call the salt and pepper shaker that launches you straight up and then throws you straight down. Actually this confessional was a little like that inside. It was tighter than most. I felt awkward and uncomfortable. Suddenly a voice from the interior darkness said, "You may begin."

"Bless me, Father, for I have sinned. It has been three years since my last confession."

"How long?"

"Three years, Father."

"Three what?"

"Years, Father. It's been three years. I know that's a long time but I've had job pressures, writing deadlines . . ."

Father interrupted me before I could go on. "Please get on with the confession. We've obviously got a lot of ground to cover." This was a bad sign—a very bad sign. There are three types of confessional priests. The first is Father Pal. He is sympathetic, understanding, and merciful. (You murdered your next door neighbor? This very serious offense is a manifestation of your need for love, communication, and understanding. For your penance please sign up for counseling with Catholic Social Services.) The second is Father Cruise. He's cruising on automatic pilot. He's heard it all a hundred times. Nothing bothers him. (You murdered your neighbor? Say three Hail Marys, three Our Fathers, and make a sincere Act of Contrition.) Third, there's Father Flog. He's old school—fire and brimstone and fifty lashes with a leather belt. Since the corporal punishment meted out to sinners by the medieval church can now be construed as a violation of state statutes, this type of priest can only conduct his floggings verbally. Obviously on this night my confessor was Father Flog. The confessional box now seemed even tighter and more uncomfortable. The thought of passing out occurred to me.

"WHAT ARE YOUR SINS?" he demanded.

"Well, Father, the usual cornucopia of human failings."

"NAME THEM," he commanded.

"Well, Father, it's difficult to remember specifics. But, you know, there's the whole gamut of sins of omission, commission, selfishness, anger, moral turpitude, irreverence...those kinds of things."

"YOU'RE NOT TELLING ME ANYTHING. CERTAINLY OVER THE PAST THREE YEARS YOU'VE GOT MORE TO CONFESS TO THAN THAT."

"Well, Father, I don't profess to be perfect. I can be a very insensitive, difficult, awful, downright terrible human being. I'm great at losing my temper and hurting people."

"I WANT SINS! I WANT SPECIFIC INSTANCES FROM THE PAST THREE YEARS WHERE YOU'VE KNOWINGLY AND INTENTIONALLY TRANSGRESSED THE LAWS OF GOD!"

"Father, I'd love to say that I murdered my sister, robbed a convenience store, or cheated on my income tax, but I'd be lying. My sins are much more amorphous than that. We don't live in a black and white world.

A long silence followed. I checked my watch. I had already been in here for fifteen minutes. At this rate I might break the Guinness World Record for the longest confession. I worried about what Michael might be thinking. He was probably imagining the worst. He was probably convinced that I had committed some terrible sins. That would be devastating because to Michael I was the All American Dad—the moral paragon. Of my three sons, he was the one who had always and unfailingly idolized me. He even wanted to be a librarian just like me. In fact that's all he talked about—libraries. Just then I heard a scratching at the confessional door and then a voice. It was Michael. "Dad," he was saying in a loud whisper, "what's wrong?"

"Michael, go away, I'm fine."

This interchange must have brought Father out of his meditation. He seemed a bit less angry with me now. "My, son," he said, "I'm going to take you over the Ten Commandments one by one."

And so that's what we did for ten minutes. We went over the laws of God. It got kind of awkward, though, at the Fifth Commandment. "Thou Shalt Not Kill," intoned Father. "Have you killed anyone?" he asked.

"No, Father," I replied. "Not in the last three years anyway."

Needless to say, Father did not find this funny. Finally, after a full twenty-five minutes, I emerged from the confessional with my sins gone and a stiff penance of prayers to say (enough Hail Marys to last an eternity). Although I had trouble adjusting my eyes to the light of the Church, I could see immediately that Michael was beside himself with anxiety.

In full view of over one hundred very attentive people he called out to me in a concerned, almost fearful voice, "DAD, ARE YOU ALL RIGHT? WHY WERE YOU IN THERE FOR SO LONG? WHAT SIN DID YOU COMMIT THAT WAS SO BAD?"

A church full of very impatient people looked up at me. They too wanted to know.

"It had to do with those library books," I said. "You were right, Michael. God does care about overdues."

He nodded his head knowingly and went into the confessional. As for me. I didn't leave the church. I just walked to the back of the sanctuary and took my place at the end of the confessional line.

After all, what I had just said was a lie—a transgression of the sixth commandment. I just hoped Father wouldn't remember my voice.

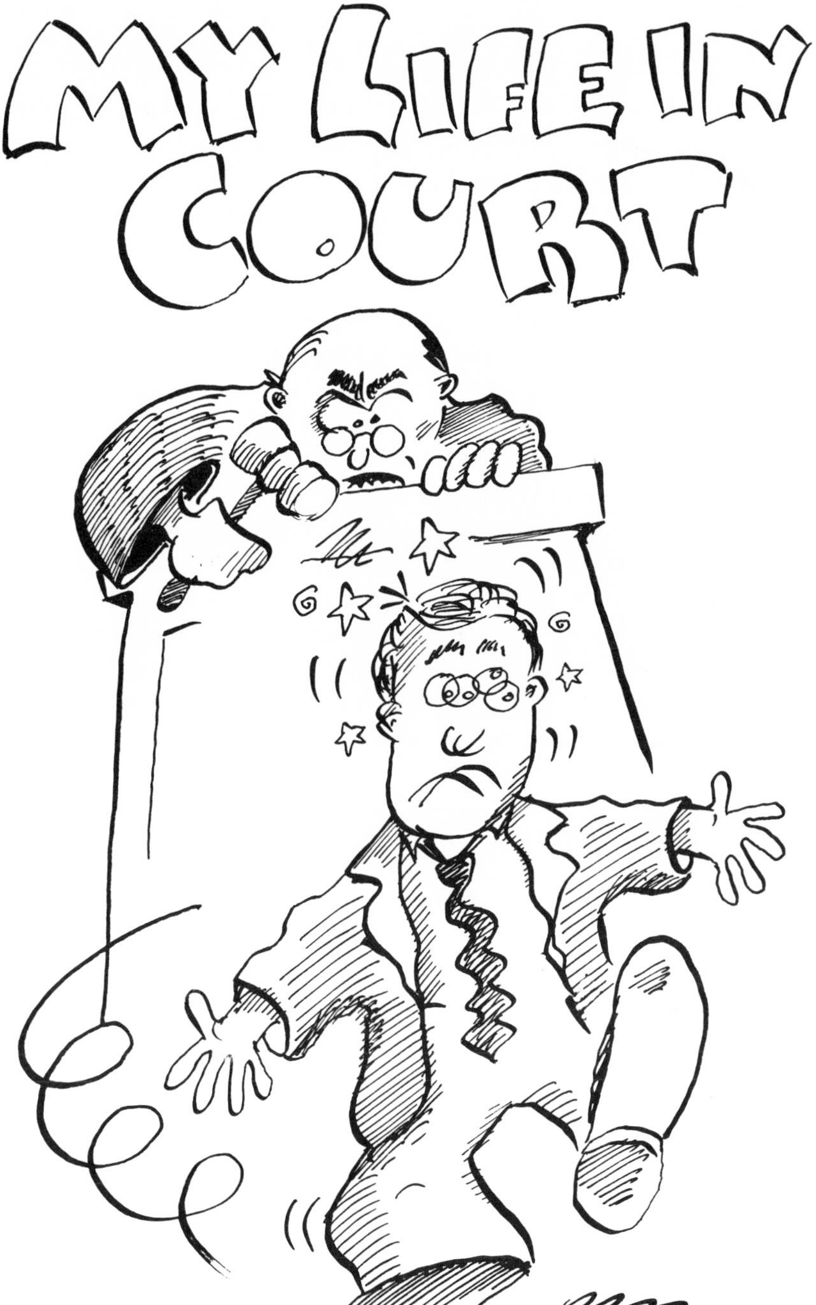
MY LIFE IN
COURT

I'm sitting in courtroom #791. It's the kind of place that gets on your nerves. The hardness of the room is what strikes you—the hard wooden tables and chairs, the hard black granite walls, the hard marbled floors. It would be nice if they could just put up one big bright painting somewhere to soften the place up. Something abstract would be nice. But there is no room for a painting because portraits of black robed justices peer down from all the walls with the disapproving scorn of Old Testament prophets.

Suddenly the judge enters. Everyone rises. He's a steely little man with a shriveled reddish face that is devoid of any promise of mercy. He's wearing plain black cowboy boots under his judicial robe. He sits down and then we all sit.

Looking up intently at the ceiling as if in search of divine guidance, he speaks loudly and ponderously: "The task before us is an awesome one. We are here to judge the guilt and innocence of a man." He pauses, peers down at the courtroom from his lofty perch with the intensity of an eagle searching for prey, and resumes: "In these weighty proceedings the selection of a jury is the first responsibility of the court. To be a juror is to fulfill the sacred bond of trust and fairness that exists between members of a democratic society. It is the greatest responsibility that citizens are given under the Constitution—greater than voting, greater than paying taxes, and greater than serving in the armed forces. It is the duty of the juror to determine the guilt and innocence of a man or a woman who has been indicted for violating the ancient contract that binds civilized men together into society." He pauses as if to ponder his own words and then continues: "As jurors you become as gods wielding the sword of judgment over the heads of your fellow man. It is not, I emphasize, a responsibility to be taken at all lightly."

He finishes speaking and looks across the courtroom where twenty of us are huddled together like frightened sheep caught in the middle of a thunderstorm. We are here because we have been told to be here by the Superior Court. We are here because, according to the Superior Court, our nonappearance will be construed as being in contempt of court, which no doubt is a violation of the ancient contract that binds civilized men together into society. We are here because we would rather be here than in jail.

Now that I am here, however, it occurs to me that the choice between jail and jury duty is not nearly so clear cut as it was when I received my letter from the Superior Court last month. After all, how long could they throw me into jail — a week, maybe two, certainly not more than three. But with jury duty Lord knows how long you could get stuck in a courtroom while your job at the library goes unattended.

As if reading my thoughts, the judge clears his throat and begins again his thunderous intonations: "The case before us is a grave one. Serious charges have been brought to bear against the defendant. This is not a simple case. The charges are numerous and complex. They involve a complicated pattern of very creative white collar crimes. This will not be a short trial."

The words echo in my mind like the sounds of an automobile accident. "This will not be a short trial." I feel like a condemned man. But why me? Why couldn't I get something cut and dried — maybe a run of the mill convenience store break-in or a minor shoplifting offense. Now I realize that I will have to resort to Strategy #2. Strategy #1 is no longer operative. Strategy #1 was to play it straight — to dutifully perform my civic duty, faithfully fulfill the greatest responsibility endowed to me under the Constitution, and judiciously wield the sword of judgment over the head of my fellow man. I would be much more enthusiastic about wielding that sword over the head of a simple smash and grab burglar than over a complex white collar con artist.

Strategy #2, therefore, becomes somewhat of an immediate necessity. Strategy #2 is best termed "proactive avoidance." According to my friend Arnold (he's a rather omniscient academic librarian at a nearby college) there are a diverse array of techniques that can be employed to avoid jury duty. "Tell them you have cancer. Tell them that your job at the library involves national security. Tell them that nine months ago you spent thousands of dollars on nonrefundable airplane tickets for a twentieth wedding anniversary trip to Pago Pago. They'll believe anything you say once you tell them that you're a librarian." When I asked Arnold where Pago Pago was, he responded, "I don't even know if it exists, but it sounds very far away."

The judge's sermon begins anew: "Let me, from the very beginning, disabuse anyone in this courtroom of any notion that I am in the habit of excusing anyone from their constitutionally ordained responsibilities for frivolous or false reasons. Such pleadings would be summarily dismissed in a most authoritative and arbitrary fashion." Pausing again to emphasize his point, he looks down at us with predatory scrutiny.

"Now," he continues, "is there anyone among you who would care to test my rather lofty standards? You would all do well to know of the hostility with which I will greet any pleas relative to trips, job responsibilities, or cancer operations. It is not that I am an unsympathetic man or even an unreasonable one. I am rather a skeptical man whose sense of mercy has been blunted by the weaknesses I have detected in the many individuals who have trafficked in my court these forty years. My view of man is not a pleasant one. Given the opportunity, men will lie, steal, procrastinate, and even murder if such acts will further their own selfish ends. Let me make it painfully clear that I will not allow anyone to perpetrate these transgressions within the sanctity of my courtroom. Let me therefore discourage anyone from violating their own integrity by warning you all that the veracity of all excuses will be thoroughly investigated. Anyone found guilty of advancing any mistruths or partial truths will be prosecuted to the fullest extent of the law. The relevant offense is called perjury." Here the judge looks up and smiles. "Now would anyone care to come forward and, under oath, and plead for a dispensation from this your constitutional duty?"

No one comes forward.

Time for Strategy #3, which according to Arnold can be called "planned eccentricity." This means that you portray yourself as an oddball, someone so strange that no prosecutor, defense attorney, or judge would want you anywhere near the jury box. "The thing is," said Arnold, "the lawyers will start asking you questions and then you will have an opportunity to get a little crazy. Don't get me wrong. I wouldn't go in there wearing a turban and chanting a mantra, but I would give them a few glimpses of eccentricity—just enough to scare them away. Lawyers love down the middle type people. They detest mavericks or free thinkers. They want sheep so don't be a sheep. Be a little weird. For instance, when they ask you for your place of residence, tell them Planet Earth. It's little things like that which drive lawyers up a wall. Predictability is what lawyers love."

At this point in the proceedings, two lawyers enter the courtroom, approach the judge's bench, and confer with him in hushed voices. After five minutes of consultation, the judge looks up at us and speaks, "There are twenty of you. By way of a process of elimination, twelve of you will be chosen for the jury. Our defense counsel and our prosecutor, after asking you a series of questions, will confer with me privately to determine who will serve as our jurors. Those of you who are not selected will be free to return to your lives."

The two lawyers walk over to the back corner of the gallery where the twenty of us are flocked together. Although both young (thirty-something), they are a study in contrasts. The defender looks like he has been surfing all week at Malibu. Sandy hair, tanned face, blue eyes, soft voice – this is a man who seems at peace with the world and with himself. He speaks freely and congenially, never groping for words and never wearing out his verbal welcome. His soothing, rhythmic cadences are a welcome respite from the judge's thunderous pomposity. His favorite word seems to be "reasonable."

The prosecutor, on the other hand, is a fidgety sort – the type of man who chews his fingers, taps his pencil, and scratches his head. A study in darkness, his hair and eyes are as black as the judge's robe. He speaks with the staccattoed force of a man jackhammering a concrete sidewalk. His favorite word is "justice."

The process is a tedious one. Each of us is asked to stand and give our name, address, and occupation. Then we are asked a series of questions. They are tedious questions: "What do you think of insurance companies? What do you think about physicians? What do you think about police officers? Do you have any strong feeling about the criminal justice system? Have you ever worked for an insurance company? Have you ever taken a law course? Do you know a man named Elmer Wooden?" The questions drone on and on.

I keep wondering where there is room for planned eccentricity. Everything is being done under the watchful scrutiny of the judge. Even during the most boring exchanges the fierce intensity of his stare never flickers. What do I say – cops are jerks, doctors are crooks, and the criminal justice system stinks? I can't say those things with old Judge Eagle Eyes looking down at me with his Old Testament "tooth for a tooth" sense of righteousness.

Finally, after two hurs, it's my turn. The beach boy has first crack at me. He says pleasantly, "Please state your full name for the record."

"William Laird Manley."

"Your occupation?"

"Librarian."

"What do you think about physicians?"

"They're nice to have around when you break your leg."

"What do you think about insurance companies?"

"They're nice to have around when your house burns down."

"What do you think about the criminal justice system?"

"It's nice to have around when your house is broken into."

Beach boy is not nearly as ticked off by the flippancy of my answers as I hoped he would be. In fact, he seems to be growing bored with his questions as well as my responses. "I have no further questions," he says pleasantly.

Now Mr. Jackhammer approaches me and says, "I have only one question." He seems to be getting tired. I sense that everyone just wants to get on with the trial. "What do you think of chiropractors?" he asks.

I can't believe it. Here is my opening, an opportunity to get a little eccentric. Without hesitating I answer, "In a word I would call them quacks. It's an insult to the medical profession that they insist on being called doctors. I wouldn't go to one even if I were dying."

"Thank you," says the prosecutor smiling. It's the first time anyone has smiled today. I take it as a compliment.

The questions have ended and once again it's the judge's turn to pontificate: "Prospective jurors, you may take a break while we confer. Please stay in the confines of the adjacent hallway and lounge."

The twenty of us are led out into the hallway. As soon as we're out of the courtroom someone approaches me and says, "Man, did you get lucky with that question on the chiropractor. They won't touch you with a ten foot pole. The rest of us are going to be stuck here forever."

Actually at this point I am feeling rather pleased with myself. The way I have it figured from all the questions is that this case involves some kind of insurance fraud relating to a car accident and that a chiropractor will be a key witness. Therefore, there's a 100 percent dead solid perfect chance that I'm going to be released by one of the two lawyers.

A woman in a uniform comes out in the hallway and asks us all to return. We troop back to the courtroom and without giving any prefatory information the judge thunders out the list of people who will serve on the jury. The name, William Laird Manley, is the first one given.

The trial ends up taking three weeks. Three weeks of fighting hot freeway traffic, three weeks of listening to the most tedious testimony you could ever imagine, three weeks of being thundered at by the judge and jackhammered by the prosecutor, and three weeks of trying to get along with eleven other people who are as testy as I am about the whole ordeal.

Finally, the last testimony is given and the last judicial oration is delivered. It is time for the us, the ladies and gentlemen of the jury, to render our verdict. This is not difficult. Every single one of us knew way back on the first day of testimony that the defendant was guilty.

Our verdict makes the judge very happy. He says in thanksgiving: "You have sent a clear message from this courtroom that crime will not be tolerated in a society of civilized people."

The bailiff then handcuffs the defendant and escorts him off to jail. I am halfway out the door when I hear the judge telling some of the jurors that they are now free to discuss the case informally with him or with the lawyers. I turn around and head for the defense attorney. This is my opportunity to discover why I had not been released during the jury selection process after my diatribe against chiropractors.

The defense attorney looks at me with a smile and says, "I wanted to eliminate you but the judge felt very, very strongly that you should stay. I let you stay because I didn't want to get the judge mad at me."

"Why did he want me on the jury?" I ask.

"Beats me. Why don't you go ask him?"

Going to see this judge, is of course, like going to Mount Sinai to meet the burning bush. I decide to chance it. It would be the fitting end to three weeks of unpleasantness. So I screw up my courage, knock lightly on his open door, and enter when he looks up.

"Mr. Manley?"

"Yes, your honor, I have a question. Why did you want me on the jury?"

"Because you are a librarian," he says matter of factly and then pauses to puff on his pipe. "And I have a high regard for librarians. They are honest, trustworthy, and intelligent. Your answer about the chiropractor confirmed that." He puffs thoughtfully on his pipe and continues, "you didn't let your profession down."

The rush hour drive is not so bad tonight. It's even tolerable. Lena Horne is on the radio singing "It Had to Be You" and there's this godly voice ringing in my ears saying, "I have a high regard for librarians."

For the first time in three weeks I'm a happy man, very happy.

HAT MAKES THE MAN

Hats, like all other types of apparel, are worn for two reasons—
functionality and aesthetics. Hats not only keep us warm and the sun
out of our eyes, they also give us instant panache.

The easiest way to achieve a certain image is to wear the right hat.
There's a hat for every occasion and attitude. It doesn't matter what
your other clothes look like, your hat defines who you are, or more accurately, who you want to be. When you wear a hat, that's the first
thing people notice about you. Hats can make a sedentary man look
rugged and a rugged man look sedentary. That's why you sometimes
see college professors wearing Australian bush hats and Mafia types
wearing fedoras.

The occupation that is most closely associated with its hat is the
construction industry. In fact the construction worker is the only person alive who is actually referred to by his hat. You rarely hear anyone
use the phrase "he's a construction worker." It's always "he's a hard
hat." It's a fitting identity. Construction workers are rough and tough.
They wear their hard hats well.

The only hat that we librarians are really associated with is what
I would call the pencil hat. It's part and parcel of the stereotype of the
little old lady with the wire-rimmed glasses, sensible shoes and hair
in the bun. Holding the bun together, of course, are the pencils. I actually once worked for a librarian like that. She carried three newly
sharpened pencils in her hair at all times. You never wanted to get too
close to her for fear of having your eyes poked out.

Other than our professional pencil heads, which I believe are the
last remnants of a dying breed, I haven't seen too many librarians sport-
ing distinctive headware. I, myself, have never been a hat person.
Hats, after all, do have their disadvantages. They mess up your hair
and you never know what to do with them once you get indoors. Also
I've never felt the desire to wear a hat for image reasons. I really don't
feel the need to look like a truck driver, a deep sea fisherman, an
English gentleman, a hunter on safari, or a Colorado mountain man.
Who knows? Maybe I got into librarianship because it's a profession
where you don't need to wear a hat.

That all changed for me, however, when my library building project went from the design to the construction phase. "Here's your hard
hat," the construction superintendent said to me early one morning.

"Anytime you come on the construction site you have to wear it.
We start work in a week."

"Yeah, right," I said nonchalantly trying to hide my enthusiasm. In reality, I was as excited about the hard hat as I was about the Philadelphia Eagles helmet that my father gave me for my tenth birthday. I couldn't wait to get home to show it to my wife and kids.

"Wow, Dad, you look neat!" is what my ten-year-old son Michael said to me when I walked into the house that night wearing my hard hat. My wife and my two older boys were not nearly as impressed. In fact they snickered. "I didn't realize that tonight was Halloween," said Stephen my fifteen year old.

My wife had a different sort of comment. "Good Lord," she said, "I hope nobody's expecting you to do any construction work on the new library. It will surely fall down if you have anything to do with it."

"Yeah," said David, my twenty year old, "whoever gave you that hard hat ought to check out the dry wall you hung in the basement."

I decided to spend the evening with Michael. After dinner, he grabbed me and my hard hat and we devoted the next hour and a half to manuevering his vast collection of toy trucks, bulldozers, backhoes, and cranes around a hill of sand and gravel. We took turns wearing the hard hat and driving the bulldozer. It was a lot of fun. "Can I get my own hard hat?" he asked.

"Sure," I answered, "I'll get you one at the hardware store tomorrow."

That weekend Michael and I spent most of our time turning the backyard sand and gravel mound into a fairly accurate facsimile of what the new library was supposed to look like. We wore our hard hats everywhere — to breakfast, lunch, dinner, and bed. The great advantage of having young children in your life is the opportunity they give you to revisit your own childhood.

Actually Michael and I accomplished more work in our sandbox over the weekend than the construction company did on the following Monday, Tuesday, and Wednesday. Those first few days were devoted solely to staking, surveying, strategizing, plotting, planning, and preparing. To be sure, there were backhoes and bulldozers on site but they sat quietly in the background like tanks and artillery poised to enter a war zone.

I used the inactivity of the first three days to strut proudly around the construction site with my hard hat on my head and a set of blueprints rolled up under my arm. I wanted everyone on the library staff to see how important I had become. I wanted them to see that I was no longer just a librarian. I was a librarian-builder, a real macho man.

By Thursday morning, however, everything changed rather radically. On my way to work that morning I could hear the roar of the bulldozers and the rumble of the backhoes from a half a mile away. The war had finally begun. The only problem was that I didn't know it was a war. I thought it was a construction project.

As soon as I got into my office I got an earful from the field inspector that we had hired. "We've got problems," he said. "These guys are getting a little overambitious. They're bulldozing the site to bits with very little regard for public safety. By contract, the entire construction site should be fenced off. They have not done that. If someone wanders out there and gets rolled over by a bulldozer, we're talking major trouble!"

"Well," I said, "please ask the superintendent to see me in my office so that we can discuss the situation and resolve the problem to everyone's satisfaction." I then pulled out my calendar and added, "I happen to have some time this afternoon."

"WILL, ARE YOU NUTS! YOU NEED TO STOP THOSE BULLDOZERS NOW! THERE'S NOTHING TO DISCUSS UNTIL THEY GET THOSE FENCES UP!"

"How do I accomplish that?" I asked with considerable nervousness.

"YOU PUT ON THAT HARD HAT! YOU CHARGE DOWN TO WHERE THE BULLDOZERS ARE! AND YOU TELL THEM TO STOP!"

"Okay," I said weakly.

"FOLLOW ME!"

I followed him. We marched over to the bulldozers and found the man in charge.

"Where are the security fences?" I asked politely.

"On order. The fencer ran out temporarily."

"You realize, don't you, that according to our contract you cannot proceed with actual construction activity until all the fences are up in their entirety?"

"They'll be up before the end of the week."

"Oh, okay," I said. "That sounds reasonable."

Then I started to walk quickly away. The inspector caught up to me. "YOU MUST STOP THEM NOW BEFORE SOMEONE GETS HURT!"

"Do I really have to?"

"YES, NOW."

"Please stop all construction activity now," I said to the construction guy. "Please."

"I told you that the fences will be up," was the answer I received.

"Look," I said, "I want to see you in the meeting room of the old library this afternoon to discuss this matter further." Then I scurried away quickly. The bulldozer was getting uncomfortably close to my face and other body parts.

The inspector was sorely disappointed in me. "You let that guy walk all over you," he said. If you don't get tough, you'll lose control of this project. You can't reason with hard hats, you have to get tough."

"It's not my way," I answered. "I employ a participative management style in the library. This is a long project. We have to work with these people for months. Yelling and screaming will only create more yelling and screaming."

"This is not the library," he answered. "It's construction. Construction is dog eat dog. If you're going to be participative you ought to wear a bonnet instead of a hard hat."

This last remark stung me. It was the first time that I realized that the hard hat I was wearing carried with it a responsibility—a responsibility to be as tough as the industry that it symbolized.

I suddenly realized that you don't put on a football helmet in order to play touch football and you don't put on a hard hat to practice Zen management philosophies.

At the construction meeting I was ready. Wearing my hard hat, I stood up, cleared my throat, and started screaming: "ALL SAFETY VIOLATIONS WILL CEASE NOW! HOSES WILL NOT BE RUN OVER SIDEWALKS! SECURITY LIGHTING THAT HAS BEEN REMOVED WILL BE REINSTALLED! AND ALL FENCING WILL GO UP IMMEDIATELY!" I did not even say "please." And for good measure, I kicked my chair and stomped out the room. There would be no participative dialog. Apparently this new approach was effective. The next day all the safety violations were promptly taken care of. Oh what a feeling!

My inspector said, "Good job, Will. I didn't know you had it in you."

To be honest I didn't think I had it in me either. It felt wonderful to win. It felt refreshing to actually wield some power. After twenty years of consensus management it felt good to order someone around arbitrarily.

After that incident, I wore my hard hat more with a feeling of empowerment than pride. I was the boss, the top dog, and king of the hill. I would talk and others would listen. The next morning a reference librarian came in and asked me if she could have the day off because her mother was dying. "Absolutely not!" I said. "You have a commitment to this institution!" Oh what a feeling. Next, a children's librarian came in. She wanted to let me know that she was going home sick. "The pros play in pain!" is the admonition I gave her. Oh what a feeling!

Wearing my hard hat home that night, I decided I had had it with my wife's new low cholesterol diet. Time to put my foot down. No more bean salads for this guy. "I HAVE HAD IT WITH VEGETABLE CASSEROLES!" I declared. "TONIGHT I WANT STEAK – A TWO INCH THICK PORTERHOUSE STEAK!"

It was a good thing I was wearing the hard hat because within a nanosecond, a rather large pyrex pot holding a rather large bean casserole landed resoundingly on my head.

"Now," said my wife, "what was it that you wanted for your dinner tonight?"

"Bean casserole," I said obediently.

"I thought that's what you said."

Oh what a feeling!

This is farfetched but if a university president were ever to approach me and say "Our institution would like to develop a graduate library school and we want you to be the dean" the first thing I would do would be to create a course called "Plaques and Certificates 101." The second thing I would do would be to require every student in the school to take the course.

There are many theories about success. Zig Ziglar says that attitude is the key to success. Norman Vincent Peale says that positive thinking is the key to success. Tom Peters says that the unrelenting pursuit of excellence is the key to success. And Donald Trump says that mastering the art of the deal is the key to success.

All of these men are wrong. The key to success in life is plaques and certificates. To prove this all you have to do is walk through the offices of successful people. Their walls are filled with plaques and framed certificates. The more successful the person is the more plaques and certificates he or she has. If life is a game then the guy who dies with the most plaques and certificates wins.

But the plaques and certificates game never ends with death. It goes on long after you die. Just walk through any graveyard and see if there isn't some sort of postmortem plaque competition going on. I've seen some cemetery monuments that are big enough to house a whole family of homeless people. Your gravestone is your ultimate plaque. You can tell everything you always wanted to know about someone by looking at his gravestone. Myself, I've been in a lot of graveyards. It seems that people I know keep dying. It has something to do with the human condition. In these graveyards I've seen all sorts off gravestones. Although most of them are engraved with floral designs, stirring prose, inspirational poetry and magnanimous epitaphs, I have seen some that are engraved with résumés and photographs of the deceased. Apparently these people think that St. Peter is going to check out their references before he lets them through the pearly gates.

And why shouldn't they think that? It's the very same approach that worked so well for them in life. Fill your office walls with plaques and framed certificates and people will be impressed. The more that people are impressed the more that you will be respected; the more that you are respected the more successful you will be.

The thing to do to be successful, therefore, is to acquire plaques and certificates. This, unfortunately, can take a long time. Only so many plaques are given out each year. One plaque that most librarians covet is the "Librarian of the Year" award that state library associations give out at their annual conference banquets. This is a very sought after plaque that requires a great deal of work and service to the profession. One librarian I know who is named Phil spent over ten years doing the kinds of things that you have to do to be nominated for the award. He joined the association, did a lot of committee work, always helped organize the annual conference, chaired the state intellectual freedom round table, and served as the association's liaison with the state Friends' group.

After ten years of this, Phil felt that he deserved to be named State Librarian of the Year, and quite appropriately was one of the two people nominated for the honor. The other nominee was a librarian who hadn't done half of what Phil had done for the profession. Phil was so confident of winning that he made all the arrangements for a big victory party for himself. He reserved a banquet room at the conference hotel, stocked the bar with a diverse array of spiritous beverages, and ordered fifty trays of finger foods.

But then something unexpected happened. Phil lost. He was so devastated by this turn of events that he packed up all the liquor and finger food into his van and took off for home at 10:00 at night. Phil lived on the other side of the state. He told me that the biggest reason why he was disappointed was because he had a perfect place on his office wall to hang the plaque.

Actually Phil had a lot of places to hang the plaque. I had been in his office many times. His walls were bare except for a framed certificate that he had received for participating in a state literacy program. Phil had made a fatal mistake. Instead of going after a number of lesser awards, Phil had focused all his efforts into winning one prestigious plaque. Even if Phil had won the award for "Librarian of the Year," it would not have made much of an impact in his office. His walls still would have been mostly barren.

Rule number one, therefore, when it comes to plaques is quantity over quality. The more plaques the merrier. This leads to rule number two, which is that no one ever reads the plaques on your walls. This is especially true when your walls are covered with plaques.

Obviously, therefore, the thing to do is to cover your walls with plaques. This can be done in one of two ways. There is the honest way and the dishonest way.

There are two main disadvantages to the dishonest route: (1) it will cost you some money and (2) you will have to change jobs to do it. Let's say you are working as a library director in Strawberry Plains, Tennessee, and you apply for a director's job in Walla Walla, Washington — 2,000 miles away. Before you move to Walla Walla there are a number of things you should do: (1) arrange for a moving van, (2) sell your house in Strawberry Plains, (3) go out and have thirty or forty plaques made in your honor.

Then when you get to Walla Walla the first thing you should do is put the plaques up on the walls of your new office in order to create the perfect ambience. When people walk through your door, they will simply assume that you have dutifully earned all these awards the old fashioned way through hard work and perseverance. Although no one will ever take the time to scrutinize all your plaques (which is kind of rude anyway) you will do well not to honor yourself with anything unnecessarily specific or outrageously important. Quell the temptation of giving yourself the Silver Star, the Congressional Medal of Honor, or the Isadore Gilbert Mudge award.

You're better off creating honors that resound with ambiguity. "For meritorious service," "In Honor of Efforts Above and Beyond the Call of Duty," and "For the Pursuit of Excellence" are the kind of things that your plaques should say. Who knows? Maybe you even deserve such high praise. The point is that no one in your new community will ever suspect that you had the gall to give yourself a roomful of honors, and not even the nosiest reference librarian would ever think to check on their legitimacy.

The biggest disadvantage with the dishonest approach is that it is dishonest, and for many of us that is an insurmountable objection. Fortunately, there are honest ways to get plaques. This can be done by volunteering for the United Way or joining a service club. These organizations are always good for two or three plaques a year. If you are a library director you can get a lot of plaques by hopping from job to job. Library boards love to give away plaques to departing library directors. I have gotten two that way. Or you could join an A.L.A. committee. American Library Association committee people love to give each other plaques. Why else would you join an A.L.A. committee?

Obviously these suggestions all take time and money, but if you are really dedicated to becoming a success in life, you'll be willing to expend the extra effort. By following these suggestions you can probably have your office walls covered with plaques in less than three or four years.

There is one sure way, however, to cut that time in half — through the ardent pursuit of certificates. In terms of impressive office decor, certificates, over the past fifteen years, have come a long way. It used to be that the only certificate you would be caught dead putting on your wall was a bona fide college diploma from a prestigious academic institution like Harvard, Yale, or Stanford.

But today things have changed. The people who run training programs have discovered the allure of an impressive certificate. Now if you sign up for a $25/two-hour training session on something like "Conflict Management" you will come away with a very nice certificate with English Gothic lettering. And you don't even have to pass an exam to get it.

Go to enough of these kinds of sessions and you can do your whole office in training session certificates, which sounds kind of unimpressive until you realize that no one can read English Gothic lettering. For all anybody knows, that Conflict Management certificate is a Dartmouth diploma. The important thing — and this cannot be stressed too much — is that you put your certificates into decent frames. Spend a few bucks. You're worth it.

The secret of success does not rest solely on your ability to get your own name on plaques and certificates. It also rests on your ability to get the names of your trustees on plaques and certificates.

In terms of plaque pecking orders, building plaques rate very, very high. There isn't a person alive who does not want his or her name on a building plaque. The only thing that rates above getting your name on a building plaque is having the building named after you. Building plaques last a lifetime. They are usually made of the most durable of materials — granite, marble, and bronze.

When I first became a library director I was very, very young, and I didn't realize how important library building plaques are to library trustees. What I discovered over time is that the older the trustee the more important the plaque becomes. A building plaque is a very tangible and impressive way to leave your mark in life. The older you get the more you want to be remembered.

At the age of twenty-nine I was too young to understand that. I learned my lesson very quickly, however, when one of my trustees asked to see a mock-up of the plaque that would be hung to com-memorate a library remodeling project.

"There are no plans for a plaque," I said genuinely surprised that he would bring the subject up.

"Whose decision was that?" he asked grumpily.

"Mine," I said. "Building plaques are usually created for newly constructed buildings, not remodeling jobs. That would be highly irregular."

"Do you want your employment here to be irregular?"

"No, sir."

"Then I suggest you rethink your decision."

"Yes, sir!"

A fellow library director told me a similar story. He was working at a library that desperately needed additional collections space. "We must expand the library," he forcefully told his trustees. Their answer was an emphatic, "Nice idea but we don't have the money."

A year later the collections problem had become unbearable. This time he took another tack with the board. "This board," he said, "is one of the most dedicated, hard working boards that I have ever been around. Regrettably, however, you are also the most unrecognized board I have ever seen. Isn't it unfortunate that the only way a board member seems to get any lasting credit in our community is by getting his or her name on a building plaque."

Long time trustee Bob Barnes then said, "Well at least Wilma Jenkins and I are on the plaque for this building. Shows how old we are I guess."

"That's nice for you and Wilma," said Jane Fredericks. "But it doesn't do anything for the rest of us."

"You know," said Harold Jennings, "I've noticed that our collection area is terribly crowded. Don't you think it's time we added on a new wing to our building?"

The board's vote was quick and unanimous. Fifteen months later all the trustees had their names in bronze.

Several years later I tried my friend's strategy with a local official who was stubbornly fighting a proposal to build a new library. "But wouldn't you like to see your name carved in granite?" I asked him.

Stubbornly he said "NO!"

Two years later when the new building was in the middle of construction he called me up. "Remember," he said, "that my middle initial is "Y".

"Why are you telling me that?" I asked absentmindedly.

"Because I want it on the building plaque."

"Oh!"

The interrogative sentence—the simple question—is often overlooked as a serious rhetorical weapon. The conventional wisdom is that questions are used solely to resolve confusion, ambiguity, and ignorance. When, for example, we ask, "Where is the post office?" we are expressing, in a very simple and straightforward way, the need for information.

But questions can also be used in a more subtle way to express strong emotions, desires, and needs. Linguistically, however, we do not live in subtle times. When we want to unleash our most ardent feelings, we tend to use simple declarative sentences spiced with the salt and pepper of profanity.

I would suggest, however, that this direct approach is becoming less and less effective. The shock value of using coarse language has diminished considerably over the last few years. Like hard-shelled insects that have grown immune to the powers of pesticides, we are no longer daunted by the force of four-letter words.

I maintain, therefore, that it is much more arresting to assault someone sneakily from the side than to try to bludgeon them with a full frontal attack. Think about it—isn't it more devastating to ask someone the question, "At what point in your life did you become a thoroughly odious human being?" than to simply call the person a four-letter word? People who attack with profanity can be dismissed as profane people, but people who can articulate their venom in the form of an intelligent question cannot be so easily disregarded.

Like any public librarian, I have found myself from time to time on the receiving end of complaints, criticism, and verbal abuse. Most of the time I have been able to handle this. It comes with the territory of working at the mercy of the taxpayers.

Patrons aren't always pleased with us when they are told that we don't carry the book they are looking for, that we don't check out reference books, and that they owe an overdue fine. Often the result is that we are called names. Sometimes the names are printable—"pigs at the public trough," "officious bureaucrats," or "inflexible cretins." Sometimes the names are not printable. Neither case does much for our egos. In response we try desperately to hold our tongue and turn the other cheek. But sometimes it is almost impossible to be entirely pacifist and so we strike back with a few choice words of our own.

Being harrassed by patrons is never a happy experience. But I'd much rather have someone call me an "officious, paper shuffling,

pointy-headed bureaucrat" than have him pop the magic question—
"Could you give me the phone number for the president of the library
board of trustees?" Those are the words that strike fear into the heart
of every library director in the world.

I first heard them eighteen years ago when I was contentedly sitting in my office computing circulation figures. My phone rang.
"Hello," I said, "this is Will."

"Yes," the caller said, "are you the library director?"

"Yes, madam, I am."

"My name is Mrs. Mary Simpson and what I want to talk to you
about is how unfairly I was treated by your circulation staff."

"Oh, that's too bad," I said trying to sound compassionate. "What
happened? Was someone rude to you?"

"Oh, no," the caller said, "the woman I talked to was very, very
pleasant. I'm sure she was just following library policy. But it was so
unfair."

"What was unfair?" I asked.

"I was charged twenty-five dollars for a book that I returned.
Somehow it got lost. But I did return it. And now they are holding me
responsible."

"I'm sorry but I can't do anything for you," I said. "If you did return
the book to the library we would have a record of it."

"Well, thank you for at least listening to my story," said the
woman. "I know that you must be very busy."

After hanging up the phone I sat back and smiled about what a
wonderfully refreshing experience it had been to have a library user
complain about an unpleasant issue in such a pleasant way with such
obvious respect and understanding. How nice it was to deal with a
patron problem without receiving insults, or threats.

These reveries about the fundamental goodness of humanity were
abruptly disturbed by my secretary who stuck her head in my door and
asked, "What's our policy on giving out the board president's phone
number?"

Absentmindedly I replied, "Give it out. He's a public official."

"Okay," she said and then headed back to her desk.

Reverting back to my usual paranoid self, I called out to her as she
was halfway down the hall, "Who wants to know?"

"A Mrs. Simpson, a Mrs. Mary Simpson," was her reply.

"OH GOOD LORD!" I exclaimed. "TRANSFER HER BACK TO ME!"

"Mrs. Simpson, hi, it's me, Mr. Manley," I said nervously.

"Oh good," she said. "Maybe you can help me, Mr. Manley. Do you happen to know the phone number of the president of the library board of trustees?"

"Mrs. Simpson," I answered, "I've been thinking maybe we ought to just forget the twenty-five dollar charge. I'll clear up the whole matter about the lost book with the circ staff."

"In that case," said Mrs. Simpson slyly, "I won't need the board president's phone number."

That little tête-à-tête took place many years ago. It was the first in a long line of strategic retreats that I have engineered as soon as someone popped the magic question on me. It doesn't matter what the issue is, I am absolutely paralyzed by anyone who threatens to go over my head.

If you want to check out two hundred books at one time; if you want to make hundreds of pages of print-outs from *Magazine Index*; if you want home delivery of your books; if you want to smoke a cigarette in the men's john; if you want us to order seventy-six books on scientology; and if you want to check *Moby Dick* out for three years all you have to do is ask the magic question, "What is the phone number of the president of the board of trustees?" That question galvanizes all of my fears and anxieties. I am absolutely paranoid about my library board getting the impression that I cannot control the day to day operation of the library.

As director, the operation of the library is my first and foremost responsibility. If patron complaints are allowed to surface to the board level in my mind it creates the impression that I cannot handle this responsibility. That is my fear, plain and simple. At all costs I want to appear to be firmly and fully in control of the library and capable of handling any situation that might arise. The irony of course is that my need to appear in control actually greatly diminishes my control.

Over the years, the people who have had the misfortune of working for me have recognized this weakness. One of my circ clerks was so frustrated by what I persistently refer to as my "managerial flexibility" that one day she paid a visit to my office. "Every time some malcontent asks for the board president's phone number," she said to me, "you fold up like a snack tray. You expect us to enforce the rules and regulations, and yet you never stand firm. We can no longer depend upon you to back us up, not even for a simple five cent fine."

"I'm sorry you feel that way," I said. "I can understand your frustration but I want you to understand the importance of staying flexible and treating each individual as a special case. Otherwise we run the risk of becoming too bureaucratic and insensitive."

"Yes, Will, I see that, but you can be flexible without giving the store away to every nut and crackpot who asks for a certain phone number. Do you know what the staff thinks of you?"

"No," I replied, "What do they think of me?"

"They think you have all the firmness of seaweed."

"To be a library director is to be misunderstood," I said philosophically.

Although I tried not to show it, that little conversation bothered me greatly. I had hoped that my spinelessness was not so conspicuous. Apparently it was. Now I was in danger of losing the support and respect of my staff, and that, I realized, could be as dangerous as losing the support and respect of the board. I knew that I was going to have to start showing some toughness.

Two weeks later the opportunity arose. A patron called me. "Those computer terminals that you have that list all of the books in the library are great. I would like one of them at home. You see, I am handicapped."

Knowing that if I gave into this outrageous demand that I would be totally discredited in the eyes of the staff, I decided to hang tough. "Sir, I said, "we just can't give you one."

"But I'm a handicapped veteran who has just had open heart surgery. Plus my wife has left me for another man."

"Sir," I persisted, "I really wish I could give you one, but I just can't. There isn't enough money in our budget to provide that kind of a service."

"Okay, Mr. Manley, I can see that you and I just don't see eye to eye. You wouldn't happen to have the phone number of the president of the library board handy, would you?"

Here was my chance to put my foot down. "The number is 578-6890. Do you have that? Let me say it again: 578-6890!"

"Thank you, Mr. Manley, and goodbye."

Saying those numbers felt great. It felt just like the time when I was ten and I got mad and hit Dogdirt Dorman, the neighborhood bully, right in the mouth. The problem was, however, seven seconds later it felt very bad when Dogdirt hit me back.

That's what I expected to happen here. Within the next three minutes I fully expected my board president to call and chew me out for mistreating a handicapped veteran who had just had open heart surgery. I was really sweating it out, but ten minutes went by and there was no call. Then a half hour went by and then an hour and pretty soon it was time to go home. Still no call.

"Tomorrow is when I will catch it," I said to myself on the way home. But tomorrow brought no fatal phone call. Over time, days stretched into weeks and weeks stretched into months, and there were still no ramifications from saying no to the handicapped vet. Now, several years later, I consider the whole thing to be a dead issue. Now I am fully confident that I will not lose my job for the tough stand that I took.

Most of all, the experience has taught me a valuable lesson. I have learned that to be a tough guy you have to be willing to pay a price. During the last few years every time my phone rang I jumped because I was afraid that it was my board president. It's awful to live in that kind of fear. I've decided I don't really want to be a tough guy. I'd much rather be a seaweed.

Yesterday, an elderly man called. He told me that he wanted the bookmobile to stop right in front of his house from 2:00 to 2:30 every Tuesday afternoon. "That's totally unreasonable," I said to him. "If we do that for you, we have to do it for everyone."

"Then you won't do it?" he asked.

"No, I won't do it."

"Okay then, what's the phone number of the president of the library board?"

"Wait a minute," I said, "I'm sure we can work something out."

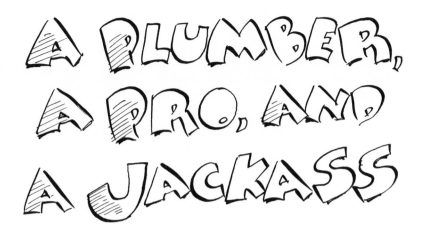

A PLUMBER, A PRO, AND A JACKASS

Recently in the middle of the night my toilet began flushing every fifteen minutes or so. My wife rolled over in bed, kicked me, and asked, "Are you all right?"

"Of course," I mumbled sleepily. "Why do you ask?"

"Because you keep going to the bathroom," she said.

I sat up in bed, looked at her, and said, "I thought that was you going to the bathroom."

"No, it's not me," she said emphatically. "I just want to get some sleep."

"Then who's using our bathroom?" I asked with some alarm.

"I have no idea!" she said somewhat hysterically. "Do you suppose someone's broken into the house?"

"What? Someone with diarrhea?" I asked skeptically.

Just then the toiled flushed again. I got up out of bed, grabbed the heavy metal paperweight that I keep on my nightstand, and headed over to the bathroom.

"Who's in there?" I asked as firmly as I could.

There was no answer.

"Come out peacefully! I am armed."

There still was no response.

Finally after ten minutes of stalling I opened the door very slowly. No one was there but the toilet flushed again. Now I was thoroughly confused. Images of poltergeists began forming in my mind. Why else was the toilet flushing? This was obviously the type of thing that poltergeists do to get your attention. But what had I done to disturb the dead? I decided to turn off the water to the toilet and return to bed.

"Don't use the toilet," I said to my wife as I settled under the covers.

"Why not?"

"Because I turned off the water to it."

"Why don't you just fix it?"

"Because it's two o'clock in the morning. Just go to sleep, will you?"

"Oh, all right," she mumbled.

The truth is it didn't make any difference what time it was. I am equally unable to fix a malfunctioning toilet in the morning, afternoon, or evening. Fixing toilets is not my strength. The next morning I did take the back of the toilet off and peered hopelessly into the various pipes and valves. I might as well have been looking at the inside of a nuclear weapon.

"I think I better call a plumber," I said to my wife. "I really can't figure out the problem."

Seven hours later a plumber appeared at my door. Besides smelling like a toxic waste dump he seemed like an amiable enough character, and it only took him twenty minutes to fix the problem.

"Here's the bill," he said. "It comes to $48.50 — $3.50 for parts and $45.00 for labor."

"What?" I asked. "Forty-five dollars for labor! That's insane!"

"That's the rate, sir."

"But you only worked twenty minutes."

"Doesn't matter," he said nonchalantly. "Anything less than an hour counts as an hour."

"Oh, here's your money," I said peevishly.

"Why didn't I marry a plumber," is what my wife said.

After that brief encounter with the plumber I suddenly had a great deal of trouble understanding why it is important to librarians to be considered professionals. I knew there was an important distinction between the terms "librarian" and "professional librarian" but for some reason I was simply unable to remember exactly why. Over the years I had read many articles about the subject but I couldn't remember anything about the articles. This was distressing because I had written some of those articles.

Like any good librarian I decided to get some clues by looking up the word "professional" in the dictionary. In his infinite wisdom here is how Webster defines professional: "of, relating to, or characteristic of a profession." Naturally I wanted to know what he had to say about the word "profession." A profession, according to Webster, is a calling that requires "specialized knowledge and often long, intensive preparation."

Now that I knew what a professional was I still couldn't understand why it was important. Under this definition plumbers, electricians, computer operators, fire-fighters, and salesmen all appeared to be professionals. In fact, in today's high tech world, it is difficult to think of many occupations that cannot, by Webster's standards, be considered professions.

"So what's the big deal about being considered a professional?" I asked one of my professional reference librarians.

She got right to the heart of the matter. "Pay," she said. "If you are considered a professional you will get more pay."

But that didn't make any sense to me because traditionally librarians have been considered professionals and plumbers have not, and yet, as my recent experience attests, most plumbers make a much higher hourly rate than most librarians. So much for pay.

So I asked another one of my professional librarians. This one was from administration. She said, "It is important for us to be professionals because of the prestige that professionalism carries with it."

But that didn't make any sense to me because it's hard to think of another occupational group that is lower in prestige than librarianship. And if you can accept my wife's comment—"Why didn't I marry a plumber?"—you would have to say that at times (when your sink is stopped up or your toilet is leaking) even plumbers with their unpleasant odors enjoy more prestige than we do.

So I decided to ask one of the librarians in the children's department why she thought it was important for us to be professionals. "Because professions have codes of ethics and it's important for librarians to have their own code of ethics," she said assertively.

But that didn't make any sense to me either. Why do you have to be a professional before you can have a code of ethics? Does that mean that if you are a plumber you are not allowed to have a code of ethics? Does that mean that plumbers are free to rape, plunder, cheat, embezzle, and murder on the job? I think not. The code of ethics argument, therefore, didn't make sense either.

This time I called up a library director from another library to get his thinking on the subject. This man said, "We insist on being called professionals so that we can form professional organizations and attend professional conventions."

But this puzzled me too because plumbers have almost as many associations and conventions as we librarians. In fact I happened to be in Las Vegas once during a plumbers convention. It looked every bit as big as the annual American Library Association conference.

Obviously the field research I was doing on this issue was getting me nowhere. Plumbers have everything that we librarians have (and more!) without the benefit of professional status. I was so thoroughly confused that I called up my friend Arnold and invited him to lunch.

Arnold is a good friend of mine from a nearby academic library. He specializes in on-line searching. He's very bright, very well read, and very in touch with the burning issues of the day. There are very few subjects that he hasn't mastered. One minute he can tell you all about Peruvian pottery and the next he can show you how to fine tune the engine on your lawn mower.

At lunch I told Arnold about my dialogue with the library staff on the subject of professionalism. "You should have come to me first," he said matter of factly.

'Then you have the answer," I asked hopefully.

"Of course," he said while wiping a crumb of French bread off his mustache. "Professionalism is a big deal for librarians for one reason and one reason only."

"What's the reason, Arnold?"

"It doesn't have anything to do with pay, prestige, ethics, organizations, or conventions. That's for sure."

"Yes, Arnold, I've already established that."

"But that's what librarians will always tell you to cover up the real reason."

"What is the real reason, Arnold?"

"The real reason is that they don't want to shelve books."

"Oh, I get it," I said. "Just like doctors won't take your temperature. There are other people that do those things. Professionals don't do menial labor. You know, Arnold, I think you're right. I once hired a reference librarian who would never, ever shelve a book. He said it was beneath him as a professional. He said that one of his library school professors told him never to shelve a book. And you know something? He never did. Not once. He wouldn't even pick up and shelve a book if it was lying on the floor right in the middle of the aisle."

"But that's not all," said Arnold.

"What do you mean?" I asked.

"There's a second part to that reason. Professional librarians don't want to shelve books but they also don't want nonprofessional library employees to answer reference questions, catalog books, or do story hours."

"I don't get it," I said with confusion. "Explain."

"Professionalism," said Arnold, "is a tool that librarians use to define and protect turf. It gives them a lofty justification for drawing lines of responsibility. It allows them to define what duties a "professional" is qualified to do and what duties a "nonprofessional" is qualified to do. More than anything, it is used to create a pecking order within libraries. There is the professional staff and there is the clerical staff and never the twain shall meet. We all want to be the top dog. Professionalism is a strategy that librarians use to achieve top dog status in their own organizations.

This explanation made me feel very uncomfortable because it hit home very hard with me. It brought back some very unpleasant memories of being a young and inexperienced library director who was determined to put his "nonprofessional" staff in their place. I felt that my fellow M.L.S. holders and I deserved a special status. It always bothered me when someone would refer to one of the circulation clerks as a "librarian." I wanted everyone to know that not just anyone could be a librarian. You had to have an advanced degree.

So the first thing I did was make it clear to my clerical staff that they were to limit their work activities to checking out books, checking in books, shelving books, and processing books. They could paste pockets on books, but they were not allowed to assign call numbers; and they could put reserves on books for patrons, but they could not recommend to them a good book to read. "Orderlies don't do open heart surgery," is how I explained it to them. This, of course, made me a very hated library director.

Reference questions were my biggest concern. I went absolutely nuts when I saw circulation clerks answering reference questions. To my way of thinking, you needed four years of college and one year of graduate library school before you could do reference. One day I really got upset when one of my circ clerks gave an answer to a patron who wanted to know where the world atlases were shelved. I waited for the man to leave before I reprimanded this employee.

"I don't want you answering any questions other than "where is the bathroom," I said sternly.

"But you don't need a master's degree to know where the atlases are kept," retorted Fay, the guilty circ clerk.

"How do you know that the patron really wants to know where the atlasses are kept?"

"Because that's what he asked for," she said firmly.

"See, that's where your lack of training can get you into trouble," I said. "Reference work is not just knowing where the atlases are shelved; it's also knowing how to negotiate the reference interview."

"I don't get it," said Fay skeptically.

"That man who asked you where the atlases are kept really didn't want to know where the atlases are kept. By telling him where the atlases are kept you gave him the wrong answer."

"Say what?" said Fay.

"That man probably wanted something else. Patrons, for one reason or another, don't tell us what they really want. They mask their real informational needs inside a very simple, innocent question. For instance that man probably is planning a trip to Capetown, South Africa. He doesn't need atlases as much as he needs extensive travel information."

"Why didn't he just say that?" asked Fay still very skeptical of my theory.

"Who knows?" I said. "Maybe he was embarrassed about traveling to South Africa because of their apartheid. Maybe he's timid about making demands on the reference librarian's time. Maybe he's afraid to reveal his ignorance about how to use the library. We professional librarians are trained to ferret that information out of the patron without embarrassing or patronizing him."

"I wish he were still here so that we could ask him," she said still unconvinced.

"The important thing for all of you circ clerks to do is to refer all questions to the reference desk," I said authoritatively.

This policy was a difficult one from the beginning. For one thing, our patrons all had their favorite library employees, and many of these favorites were in the circulation department. Years of greeting people and checking out their books had made the circulation staff very popular with the public. Consequently when our regular patrons needed something they often went directly to the circ staff, the people with whom they felt most comfortable. Obviously someone had forgotten to tell our patrons about the importance of having an M.L.S. when negotiating a reference interview.

Two things happened. When I was out of sight the circ clerks would surreptitiously answer the patrons' questions, and when I was in sight (usually at the reference desk), they referred the patrons to me. This naturally got many of the patrons very mad. But professional standards are professional standards, and I was bound and determined to uphold professional standards. I had only been out of library school for a few short years.

One Saturday, a patron hurried up to Fay at the circulation desk.

From my vantage point at the reference counter I could see that this man was very agitated and that his pants were damp. He spoke to her in a rather loud and urgent voice.

"Fay, my toilet is leaking like a sieve. I've got to fix it right away since it's the only toilet in the house. Could you tell me what to do."

Fay, who had a reputation around town as a very knowledgeable handywoman, often was asked this type of question. If she didn't know the answer she knew where to find it. Her knowledge of the home repair books was very thorough probably because the previous library director allowed her to select books in that area. Fay looked at the patron and then at me. "Elwood, you'll have to ask Mr. Manley. He's the reference librarian on duty today."

"That's all right," he said, "you can just tell me."

"No, Elwood, I'm not allowed to answer your question because I don't have an M.L.S."

"What's the Multiple Listing Service got to do with this?" he asked. "I DON'T WANT TO SELL MY HOUSE JUST BECAUSE THE TOILET DOESN'T WORK! I JUST WANT TO FIX IT! I DON'T NEED A REALTOR!"

Elwood was obviously all worked up so I ambled over and introduced myself. "I'll be glad to help you," I said pleasantly.

"I have a badly leaking toilet," he said. "I need to know how to fix it."

"Are you sure that's really what you need," I said beginning my reference interview.

"YES, THAT'S REALLY WHAT I NEED!"

"Well, Elwood," I said, "Let me walk you over to the plumbing books. We have an excellent collection. In fact here's a good one right here," I said pointing to a relatively new home plumbing book with attractive color illustrations. "Take this and follow the simple directions given in the chapter on toilets."

Elwood tucked the book under his arm like a fullback carrying a football, checked it out, and rushed out the door. On my daily reference report sheet I made a nice, neat check-mark under the category "Reference Questions Answered Correctly." I also flashed a triumphant look of self satisfaction over toward Fay at the circ desk. She was not amused.

Six hours later, right before closing time, Elwood reappeared. He looked tired, frustrated, and testy. His pants were now more than damp. They were wet. He came over to me and said, "YOU TRY FIX-ING A TOILET WITH THIS BOOK!" Then he slammed the book on top of the reference counter and deposited an array of washers, screws, and plumbing parts on top of my daily reference report sheet.

"Did you have a problem?" I asked gingerly.

"YES!" he said. "MY TOILET DOESN'T LOOK ANYTHING LIKE THE TOILETS IN THIS BOOK!"

Just then Fay ambled over. "Let me see that book," she said picking it up and leafing through it. Suddenly she put it down with a thud and looked straight at Elwood and then at me. "The book you gave him is a British publication that you obviously got from that crooked remaindered salesman friend of yours. British toilets don't work like American toilets!"

"Oh," I said quietly and with a great deal of humility.

"I'M MAD NOW!" declared Elwood, "I'M REAL MAD! IT'S TOO LATE TO CALL A PLUMBER!"

"Don't be mad, Elwood" said Fay. "I get off the desk in fifteen minutes. I'll be glad to come over and fix your toilet for you."

"Thanks, Fay," said a greatly relieved Elwood. "You're one in a million." Then he looked at me and said, "Young man, you're really lucky to have someone like Fay working for you. She's a real pro, isn't she?"

"Yes, Elwood, she is. She's a real pro. And I'm a real jackass."

CRUEL AND UNUSUAL PUNISHMENT

What do librarians do in their leisure time?

We do a lot of different things. Some of us collect coins, some of us play golf, and some of us hang glide. But probably our most popular leisure time activity is complaining about local politicians.

The simple fact of the matter is that most librarians do not feel loved, valued, appreciated, or understood by most politicians. To the average librarian, the average politician is an unschooled, closeminded tightwad.

In our low regard for politicians, we librarians are no different than any other type of professional working in the public sector. Teachers, nurses, doctors, lawyers, city planners, engineers, policemen, and fire fighters all feel the same way about politicians. They are ranked somewhere above ax murderers who kill their mothers.

Politicians are the most criticized people in the world. "Throw the rascals out," is the rallying cry of the American people at election time. But then what happens? We throw the rascals out and then we ask their replacements to perform the magical act of giving us cradle to grave government services without raising any taxes to pay for them. When these new rascals fail to perform the obligatory miracles we are quick to castigate them for being stupid, crass, insensitive, and dishonest. Sometimes when I hear one of my fellow librarians refer to a city councilman or county commissioner as an "uneducated functionally illiterate and culturally backwards cretin" I wish I could put that librarian into the cretin's moccasins for just a day.

It would be a shock. I know. I once ran for public office and had the misfortune of winning. It happened many years ago. I can't quite remember exactly why I ran but I do remember that at the time it seemed like a good idea. No doubt I was impelled by the same blend of idealism, naïveté, and egotism that motivates many other political candidates.

The office I ran for was a seat on a school board in a school district that was in a terrible financial pickle. There were six of us who decided to compete for the three open seats. A friend of mine described the campaign as six crazy people fighting for the opportunity to take a one way trip to hell.

It was an interesting experience. The main campaign issue was money—pure and simple. There was just not enough of it in the district treasury to keep all the schools open. At least five or six schools would have to be closed. There are very few things more traumatic than closing a school. Closing a school goes against the moral grain of every red blooded American. Ours is a country that worships the virtues of public education. Closing a school, therefore, is a lot like burning a Bible. But there were six of us who were willing to fight for the opportunity. We were basically identified by our occupations. I was the librarian candidate.

When the campaign began, I had no campaign war chest. "Just remember," my wife warned me, "every dime you put into your campaign is a dime you take away from your three children." I decided to run a cost free campaign. I wasn't so nuts that I was willing to pay for the opportunity of closing schools.

At the beginning of the campaign it was my belief that the five of us who were running did not like each other all that much. We may not have been enemies, but we certainly were not friends. As the campaign evolved, however, that began to change. We began to like each other and sympathize with each other. "What are we getting into?" is what we began asking each other the more we got into the campaign. It was no fun trying to answer impossible questions like: "How will you improve education, increase teacher salaries, and keep all the schools open without raising taxes?"

Everyone—teachers, parents, and concerned taxpayers—looked upon us as the heroes who would make everything right. Naturally at first it was flattering to be thought of as a hero who could step in and do the impossible. So instead of telling the truth I willingly joined in the deception that you could save the district without tax money. Basically I told people what they wanted to hear. Ronald Reagan at the time was my role model, and voodoo economics was very much in vogue.

Not until nosy newspaper reporters began to ask me embarrassing questions about my miracle plan did I honestly regret throwing my hat in the ring. That's when I began to look at my rival candidates with greater respect. "You know," I told my wife, "any of the other five candidates would make great school board members. Maybe I ought to just drop out." She was a harsh counselor. "You made a commitment" was her unfriendly advice.

Mercifully, after countless candidate forums and appearances before teacher groups, parent groups, and civic clubs, election day arrived. Up until that morning my attitude toward the election continued to be lukewarm—"If I win, fine; if I lose, thank God."

But that quickly changed when I closed the curtains of my voting booth and saw my name on the ballot. My pride was at stake. I suddenly realized that I didn't want my wife, my kids, my neighbors, my parents, my in-laws, and all the people at my library to see me as a loser. When you get right down to it, no one in America loves a loser and no one in America loves to lose (with the possible exception of Cubs fans). So I pulled down the lever next to my name with great conviction. "At least I will get one vote," is what I told myself. My wife told me that she was voting for someone else. She told me that "his ideas on gifted education are better than yours."

That election day turned out to be the longest day of my life. At first I wanted to lose. Then when I saw my name on the ballot I decided that I wanted to win. Then I decided that I wanted to win big. Then I decided I would settle for a close but decisive win. Then I decided that I would be happy to win by one vote. Then I decided that it would be okay to lose if I at least made a respectable showing. Then I decided I would be satisfied with 200 votes. Then when the polls were closing I decided that I could keep some semblance of pride with a hundred votes. That was my bottom line. Anything less would make me look ridiculous. A half hour later when the votes were being tallied I decided that the respectability threshold was really closer to fifty votes. If I could get fifty votes I would not be totally humiliated. By 9:00 P.M. I was a basket case. At 11:00 P.M. the people on the local radio station were declaring me one of the three winners. I had finished third. My pride and dignity had been preserved.

Thereafter, the phone calls began. "Congratulations, Will!" exclaimed one of my reference librarians. "You've done our profession proud."

"Piece of cake," I said with a swagger. "I knew I had it all the way — wasn't a bit nervous."

"Congratulations!" said another caller.

"Never a doubt!" I responded with euphoria.

"Congratulations, Will!" said the next caller. "I want to invite you to meet with parents of handicapped students tomorrow morning at 6 A.M. We all voted for you and now we think you need to get acquainted with our concerns about the way our children are being treated by the district."

"Six A.M.?" I asked with a noticeable lack of euphoria. "I guess I can make it."

That was the last call I got that night, but the next day and for everyday thereafter for the entire duration of my term of office, my phone rang and rang and rang. If the issue wasn't handicapped children, it was head lice or inappropriate reading materials or disciplinary hearings or gifted education or sex education or corporal punishment or rude bus drivers or incompetent teachers or psychotic janitors or broken teeter-totters or school building graffiti. People would call me in the morning, afternoon, evening, and even in the middle of the night ("I thought I could get a hold of you at this hour"). They would call me on weekdays and weekends, at work and at home.

But that was not the worst part. The worst part was that everyone who called me had the same line: "Will, I expect you to do something about this problem immediately. Remember, Will, I voted for you. You owe me." This type of emotional blackmail disgusted me. If so many people had voted for me why did I finish third? With each succeeding phone call I got testier and testier. Finally I lost it.

"Will, you really need to do something about Mrs. Trotter. She's my daughter's third grade teacher. She insists that my daughter should be in the lower reading group and I think she's wrong. Please do something, Will. Remember, I voted for you."

"Did you really vote for me?" I asked.

"Yes," he said.

"That decides it," I said. "In my eyes you are the culprit. You put me into this thankless office. No, I won't do anything about Mrs. Trotter!"

"Well, don't worry, Will. Next election I won't vote for you."

"THAT'S RIGHT," I said. "NEXT ELECTION YOU WON'T VOTE FOR ME BECAUSE YOU WON'T FIND MY NAME ON THE BALLOT!"

There's a lesson here. If you really want to punish your enemies in a cruel and unusual way, just vote them into public office.

I've decided that the three most important things in life are your family, your religion, and your carpeting. That carpeting could worm its way into this trinity of American values is really quite amazing because there are very few things in life that are more illogical than the concept of carpeting.

Think about it. In a rational world wouldn't it make sense that you would put your most durable materials on the floor. Stone floors, tile floors, and even wood floors make sense from an appearance, durability, and maintainability standpoint. So what in our rational world do we irrational people do? We cover our floors with fabric — fabric that will get quite dirty, worn, and unseemly in only a few weeks or months.

The absurdity of carpeting hit me at a very young age when I was playing at a friend's house and began to wander into his living room. "YOU CAN'T GO IN THERE!" his mother screamed with terror as if I were about to commit an ax murder.

"Why?" I asked innocently.

"BECAUSE THAT'S OUR LIVING ROOM!"

"What?" I said confused.

"YOU'LL MAKE FOOTPRINTS IN THE CARPETING!"

This interested me. The idea of making footprints in the carpeting sounded like great fun to me, almost as much fun as making footprints in the snow. So as soon as my friend's mother left, I headed right for the living room and made footprints to my heart's content. Unable to resist the fun, my friend dropped his inhibitions and joined in. When his mother returned, however, he was grounded for a time period somewhat short of eternity.

But this woman was not out of the ordinary. A good portion of my boyhood memories have to do with trying to stay out of people's living rooms. "DON'T TRACK UP THE CARPETING!" is one of the top three motherly warnings in America. It ranks right up there with "DON'T PRESS YOUR NOSE AGAINST THE WINDOW!" and "DON'T PUT PLAY DOUGH IN THE TOILET!"

The reason for this is simple — carpeting looks great when it is first installed. It is not until people actually start walking on it that it begins to look rather depressing. Ninety-five percent of the carpeting in America looks disgusting. The other five percent, like my friend's living room, is kept off limits to pedestrian traffic.

Library carpeting is even worse. Ninety-nine percent of it looks disgusting; the other 1 percent is in buildings that have not yet been opened to the public. And yet, there's not a library in the country that is not carpeted. As an architect once told me, carpeting creates a warm, friendly, and quiet environment—perfect for a library.

There is, however, one very big problem with library carpeting. It is difficult, if not impossible, to replace. The cost of moving everything out of a library in order to put new carpeting down can be almost as expensive as the new carpet itself. It is also a very time consuming process that can require a library to shut down for a week or even longer.

Because of the cost, downtime, and the chaos of moving, most library directors will do anything to avoid recarpeting. I have even heard of directors who have had their old carpeting dyed before they would consider having new stuff put in. But the unfortunate truth is that recarpeting, like death, potholes, and car repairs, is inevitable.

I knew that it was time to redo my library when, after twelve years, there were more bald spots than carpeted spots on the floor. You could actually see more of the jute backing than the nylon fibers. It was not a pretty sight. However, I will say that the jute backing wore very well. If only the carpet were as durable.

Library recarpeting jobs start with the competitive bidding process. Another name for this is war. Public libraries, unlike private companies, must award contracts to low bidders. If you were going to carpet yourown house you would select the carpeting firm that you felt would do the best job. As a public library director, however, you are pretty much obligated by law to select the firm that will do the cheapest job. This, of course, can be a disaster—not always but sometimes. At the very least it is risky business. Fortunately, carpet installation is not heart surgery.

Once you have written your job specifications, sent them out to potential bidders, and gotten back all your bids, the war begins. Before you actually award the contract to the low bidder, the higher bidders go on the attack. Their strategy is to discredit the low bidder by calling into question his competency, integrity, and moral character. The accusations will range from "He is a psychopathic murderer who is on the F.B.I.'s Most Wanted List" to "His company is two weeks away from bankruptcy and the Environmental Protection Agency is going to shut him down."

As the librarian in charge you are naturally concerned about all these allegations. Since you do not want a criminally violent, bankrupt polluter installing your carpeting, you naturally have a responsibility to do some investigation. With your budget and deadline, however, about all you can do is call the low bidder up and ask him if he is a criminally violent, bankrupt polluter. Just for the record, the answer is always an indignant "No!" So you pray.

Fortunately, in my particular case, my prayers were answered. My carpet guy turned out to be a morally solid and financially sound individual. But I realized that was only half of the battle. There was still a job to be done. Every single book and stick of furniture had to be removed from the library, the old carpeting had to be ripped out, the new carpeting had to be installed, and then every book and stick of furniture had to be put back into place. All of this had to be done in seven days.

I was fairly optimistic until the first minute of the first day. That's when twenty or thirty ragtag college students showed up at my front door in their tee shirts, cutoffs, and sandals. I quickly learned from my carpet man that they were to be my movers. I had expected Mayflower, Van Lines, or Bekins. Instead I got Larry, Darryl, and Darryl. Thinking back to my own college days, I would have preferred prison labor. I was not completely thrilled about the prospect of these kids moving 250,000 books and 20,000 pieces of furniture and equipment. In that first moment of that first day I knew it was going to be a long week.

I was not wrong. Within two hours I was hoarse from yelling things like "COMPUTER TERMINALS ARE NOT SOCCER BALLS!" "YOU ARE NOT GETTING PAID TO PLAY TOUCH FOOTBALL WITH THE CRISS CROSS DIRECTORY," "510.993 COMES BEFORE 515!" "YOU MUST TIGHTEN ALL THE SUPPORT WIRES ON THE STEEL SHELVING! DO YOU WANT TO KILL SOMEONE?" "NO, I DON'T WANT TO CHANGE THE LOCATION OF THE CHILDREN'S FICTION DEPARTMENT!" and "NO, YOU SHOULD NOT THROW AWAY THOSE OLD, DOG-EARED BOOKS! THAT'S OUR LOCAL HISTORY ARCHIVES!"

By Wednesday I was clutching a set of rosary beads and saying multiple Hail Marys. I had a great fear that somehow thousands of books were going to be lost during the move. I could just imagine my next library board meeting when the trustees discovered on their monthly report that in a one-month period our collection had shrunk from 250,000 volumes to 150,000 and I would have to say, "Obviously, our new aggressive weeding policy has been very effective."

By Friday night I had graduated from saying rosaries to conducting full scale novenas. Not only were we going to lose 100,000 books but half of our furniture was going to be lost, broken and stepped on. "That old furniture," I would have to say to the board, "looked totally inappropriate with the new carpeting."

By Sunday afternoon, I had reached the all time low point of my spiritual life. I was reduced to divine groveling. "Oh my God," I beseeched, "if by tomorrow morning at 9:00 A.M. every book, table, and chair is back in place, I will never, ever ask You for another favor again in my life. Furthermore, God, from now on all my prayers will be devoted to noble causes such as preserving world peace, saving the ozone layer, and keeping Liz Taylor out of the tabloids."

Thank God for miracles. Two minutes before opening on Monday morning, every book and every stick of furniture was back in place, and I could be found wandering around the library saying, "Praise the Lord, praise the Lord."

"I'm taking him home," is what my wife said to the library staff.

For two months my library life was heavenly. I was back to the pleasureable routine tasks of writing board reports, attending library director meetings, and watering my office philodendron. Life's simple pleasures are never fully appreciated until after an earthquake.

And then one day when I was contentedly proofreading the latest library monthly report ("the library recarpeting job turned out to be a very challenging but very successful endeavor") my maintenance man came in to see me.

"Will, the new carpeting is falling apart."

"What?"

"The new carpeting is falling apart."

"Where?"

"The adult nonfiction area."

"Go away."

He went away.

It took me a half hour but I finally worked up enough courage to walk out to the adult nonfiction area. The carpeting was fuzzing up into big balls of fiber.

It did not take too long for the entire carpet to be infected with this fuzzy disease. Something had to be done. A lawyer was called in.

The lawyer took a good look at the fuzzy carpet and said, "There is a very good chance that if you sue, you will win."

"What happens if we win?" I asked.

"They will have to come back, move everything out of the library, rip up the old carpet, install the new carpet, and move everything back in."

After a couple of minutes of silence, the lawyer looked up at me and asked, "So, do you want to sue?"

"No!" I said emphatically.

This took the lawyer by surprise. "What's wrong?" he asked. "Are you afraid of losing?"

"No," I said, "I'm afraid of winning."

CATALOGERS AND CATALOGING
Myths, Misunderstandings and Perversions

An old library school professor of mine used to say over and over again that in practicing the art and science of Anglo-American cataloging, appearances can be deceiving. *Moby Dick* was the example that he frequently used to make his point. "*Moby Dick*," he used to say, "might appear to be a book about whales and whale hunting but that book is no more about whales than *The Catcher in the Rye* is about baseball." And then he would lean over to us and in hushed tones, as if he were letting us in on some great cosmic secret that no one else should know about, he would whisper, "It is a book about God."

His point was that you have to look beyond titles, dust jackets, publisher's blurbs, and book reviews to find out what a book is really about. In his opinion, books are organic; they are living things. You have to spend time with them. "Pick them up and poke at them," he used to say.

The same advice is applicable to catalogers themselves. As a class of people they are not nearly as easy to catalog as we might think. The common temptation is to classify them as human plant life. After all, the accepted view is that they seem to prefer not to have a lot of excitement in their lives.

At first glance, catalogers do appear to be excessively shy, quiet, and serious. "Wallflower" is the term that most readily comes to mind. But for some people in our profession "wallflower" is not a strong enough word with which to describe catalogers. There are a significant number of librarians (mainly in public services) who believe that catalogers are not just shy but socially dysfunctional, that they have certain anal retentive characteristics that render them incapable of engaging in normal, healthy interpersonal relationships. Sometimes the word "misanthropic" is thrown in.

The bias against catalogers stems from the nature of their work. Theirs is a quiet, solitary labor carried on in the library's shadowy periphery. More often than not, they ply their trade in the least desirable locations in the library building. Frequently you will find them working busily away in damp basements, dusty backrooms and dreary mechanical areas. The relegation of catalogers to such drab, windowless work spaces is often more evolutionary than intentional.

The choicest and most attractive spaces in the building are naturally reserved for the public. The public always comes first. This is as it should be. But what happens through the ebb and flow of time is that new libraries get busier and busier, shelves get more and more crowded, and sooner or later the cataloging room is invaded by the reference or children's department under the pretense that the public needs more space. As a consequence the catalogers are forced to retreat deeper and deeper into the inner recesses of the building.

Not only do catalogers have to endure inferior working conditions, but they also have to suffer the indignity of being defined by these working conditions. The common myth is that just because catalogers work in drab, windowless areas they actually prefer these conditions. The truth is catalogers are not some weird species of human silverfish. Darkness and dampness are no more their natural habitat than filth and squalor are the habitat of our urban poor. Catalogers are victims of circumstance. They do not seek out darkness, but when asked to make organizational sacrifices, they willingly cooperate. Just because they are thrust into unpleasant places does not mean that they enjoy them.

Of course, environments do change people and it is possible that by being isolated into unpleasant work areas, an aura of social aloofness can develop around catalogers. After all, what reference librarian wants to walk down a flight of stairs to a depressing basement room just to be able to shoot the breeze about added entries with one of the catalogers. The aloofness in that case, however, is all the fault of the reference librarian, not the cataloger. But through some weird form of twisted logic we accuse the cataloger of being antisocial.

The nature of the cataloger's work is also subject to misunderstandings. The conventional wisdom is that librarians who do not like people go into cataloging specifically so that they can work alone. If they were "people" persons they would go into public services. But obviously they would rather spend time with a computer terminal than with human beings. The fallacy here, however, is the assumption that catalogers are not interested in helping library patrons.

This is nonsense. No one on the library staff does more to help patrons than catalogers. In any library, the single most important component, other than the book collection, is the catalog. Without the catalog, the book collection loses 99 percent of its useability (in larger libraries this percentage increases to 99.9 percent). Even the most gifted reference librarian is professionally impotent without a catalog. Catalogers are, therefore, the consummate public services librarians even though the reference librarians get all the glory.

This is not to say, however, that catalogers are the world's most wonderful people. Unfortunately, like us all, they do have some very disconcerting idiosyncrasies. Specifically, they can be annoying, very annoying. This quality was best explained to me by a cataloger, herself. The occasion was a job interview. I was considering this woman for a position in my cataloging department and asked her very directly, "As an employee what is your biggest weakness?"

"That's easy," she replied. "I'm perfect."

"No, you misunderstood," I said. "I asked for your biggest weakness. "We'll get into your strengths later on."

"No, I didn't misunderstand," she said assertively. "My biggest weakness is that I'm perfect."

"I don't get it," I said.

"Let me explain," she said. "I do perfect work but that's a problem because it makes everyone else look bad. They resent it."

"Oh," I said. "Now, what is your biggest strength?"

"I'm perfect!"

"Oh."

That's precisely what makes me nervous about catalogers. They often are perfect. Remember that girl in high school who always ruined the grading curve in chemistry class by getting perfect scores? She grew up to be a cataloger. And that roommate you had in college who always made his bed, picked up his side of the room, and flossed his teeth three times a day — remember him? Well, he became a cataloger too.

That woman I interviewed was right. Perfect people are rather impossible to live with. They're constantly correcting your grammar, buckling your seat belt, and straightening your tie. You can't relax around them, and every once in a while you want to strangle them. That's not to say, however, that perfect people aren't handy to have around. I'm particularly in favor of having them run nuclear power plants, pilot airplanes (especially the ones I'm on), and perform open heart surgery (especially mine).

But I do have a problem when perfectionism is wasted on something so mundane as the art and science of Anglo-American cataloging. I mean who really cares if a comma gets misplaced or an author's name gets transposed. The ground won't shake and rumble and the skies won't thunder and roar over a stray hyphen or a renegade colon. It's not that important. But to a cataloger it is.

One of the professors who introduced me to the intricacies of

AACR2 was so severe in his standards of perfectionism that he some-times reduced students to tears over an incorrect publication date or an inaccurate classification number. He once used a phrase — "colon abuse" — that at first confused me because I thought it described a medical condition. Not so. For him it meant the "wanton disregard for the rules governing the proper bibliographical application of colons (punctuation marks)." He talked like that.

Colons were his big pet peeve. God forbid if someone should put a colon where a comma should be. His face would redden, the veins in his neck would pop out and pulsate, and he would start screaming, "THE HORROR, THE HORROR." That was a strange expression. He got it straight out of the *Heart of Darkness* — the part where a dying man is reflecting on all the despicable acts that he has perpetrated in the jungle — murder, cannibalism, and slavery. Somehow I thought the phrase was just a little overdone when applied to the improper use of colons in bibliographical applications.

Later on, the phrase made a little more sense when it was rumored that this professor was one of the foremost authorities in the world on the utilization of colons in Anglo-American cataloging. Apparently sometime in the 1950s, when this guy was in his heyday, this was a hot topic. The funny thing was that even though this guy jackham-mered colons into our heads with such violence, I can't remember one whit about them. My position on the subject has always been if it feels really right to use a colon then use it. Otherwise stay away from them. They are trickier than a knuckleball on a breezy day.

But the colon question is just one small part of the confusing swirl of controversies that make cataloging such an unpleasantly com-plicated use of human intelligence. There are many other concerns such as the use of the comma, the period, and the semicolon (which I always considered to be a kind of younger brother of the colon). But, in my opinion, all of these issues take a backseat to the most vexing dilemma of all — the distinction between a dash and a hyphen.

More substantive, but equally frustrating, were the class discus-sions on subject headings. What was the point of arguing the rela-tive merits of the headings KOREAN WAR or KOREAN CONFLICT? To me it was nothing more than academic hair splitting, and I didn't get into librarianship to be an active participant in such obvious non-sense.

Twenty years later, still seething with bitterness from this class,

I vented all my frustrations about catalogers and cataloging into a scathing diatribe for the *Wilson Library Bulletin*. The response to this heavy handed polemic against catalogers was fascinating. Many people wrote to thank me for my bravado. I had apparently expressed their own deep seated contempt for cataloging. These letters, however, were unsigned and contained no return address. For reasons I could not understand these librarians all wanted to remain anonymous.

And then there was the other response — the flood of letters attacking me for my mean spirit, my utter lack of professional sophistication, and my deplorable ignorance about cataloging in the age of the computer. Although these letter writers angered and shamed me, they did end up changing my thinking about catalogers. Their arguments were spirited, informed, and convincing. But more importantly they all had the courage of their convictions — all the letters were signed and some of them were even intended for publication.

The whole rather unpleasant controversy motivated me to radically rethink my views. These catalogers were basically saying: "Wake up. Our work has to be precise and exacting. We don't enjoy nitpicking and hairsplitting any more than you do. All we are interested in is providing the best possible access to every single book in our libraries. If we make a mistake, the book is lost. You might as well throw it away."

The remorse I felt about writing my unprovoked attack on catalogers intensified to the point that I even picked up a copy of AACR2 and began to leaf through it. I hadn't done this since my days with Professor Colon. It was, however, like visiting the scene of a very bad car accident. My stomach tightened and the old feelings of nervous anxiety returned. Once more, commas, colons, dashes, and hyphens began swirling painfully around in my head. To quote Yogi Berra: "It was déjà vu all over again." I quickly slammed the book shut and hurried away from it like it was a bomb ready to go off.

I knew that I was still not cut out to be a cataloger. Twenty years and a spate of angry letters didn't change that reality. And yet despite my own personal revulsion from the work of cataloging, I was at least beginning to acquire an appreciation for catalogers in much the same way that I was able to appreciate accountants and dentists. Furthermore, in a world in which language has been devalued and traditional standards of grammar were being desecrated, I was beginning to appreciate the exacting standards prescribed by AACR2.

Within this context of renewed respect, I had to make some decisions about the catalogers in my own library. How much did I value them? The question was very pressing because I was designing a new library and I wasn't quite sure about what to do with the catalogers.

My head of technical services had no doubts about the matter. "Let them have light," he said over and over again. "Catalogers are not second class citizens. They should not be banished to darkness. If anyone needs a window for visual relief, it is the poor cataloger. This is a person who sits at a terminal all day long." I decided he was right. The catalogers should have windows. "That will cost you extra money," warned the architect. "So what," I said, self-righteously. "Catalogers need light!"

When you build a public library building there are always surprises when it is done. Ceiling heights, lighting levels, and building angles often appear quite differently from how you imagined them in the architectural drawings. But even more surprising is the reaction of the public to the building — "it's so big, it's so stark, where's the front door?" The biggest surprise I had in my building, however, was the controversy over the catalogers' windows.

We hadn't been open long before the calls started:

"I OBJECT TO THOSE WINDOWS ON THE WEST SIDE OF THE BUILDING!"

"MY NEIGHBOR AND I ARE GOING TO FILE SUIT AGAINST THE LIBRARY FOR INVADING OUR PRIVACY!"

"WHY WEREN'T WE WARNED THAT THERE WOULD BE WINDOWS ON THE SECOND FLOOR OF THE WEST SIDE OF THE BUILDING!"

'THERE ARE PERVERTS IN YOUR LIBRARY WHO ARE LOOKING INTO MY HOUSE. TELL THEM TO STOP!"

In all, I took ten calls, which is logical because there are ten houses that back up to the west side of the library. The three offending windows which loomed above their homes were, of course, the catalogers' windows. I obviously had made five catalogers very happy and ten sets of homeowners very unhappy.

Naturally, the first thing I did was go over to the windows and peer out to check the extent of the problem. This was a relief. Because we had put a six foot brick wall and a double row of trees on the west property line, the visual intrusion was minimal. The backs of the houses were clearly visible, but you definitely could not peer down into the neighbors' backyards or swimming pools.

My strategy, therefore, was to invite all the neighbors over to check out the view themselves and meet our catalogers to see for themselves that they were not perverts who would want to peep into their houses.

Soon everything died down.

Almost.

Faithfully every afternoon between 2:00 and 5:00 I got a call from an elderly woman who always refused to give her name or address. Each conversation went like this:

"YOUR CATALOGERS ARE PERVERTS! THEY KEEP LOOKING DOWN INTO MY HOUSE!"

"Are they doing it now?"

"YES!"

"Hold on. I'll go tell them to stop this instant." Then I would put down the phone and race over to the cataloging workroom. The catalogers, of course, would be pecking busily away at their terminals. "Madam, I just checked. They're not looking out the windows. They're working at their desks."

"THAT'S JUST BECAUSE YOU TOLD THEM TO STOP. THEY ARE PERVERTS. I HAVE NO PRIVACY IN MY HOUSE! THEY ARE DRIVING ME CRAZY! I AM GOING TO KILL MYSELF!"

"Oh please don't do that," I would plead. "Please come over to my office. I will be happy to introduce you to my catalogers. You will see that they are very nice people."

"THEY ARE PERVERTS! I WON'T GO NEAR THEM!"

Every morning I was afraid to look in the morning paper for fear that the headlines would read — WOMAN KILLS SELF; BLAMES PEEPING CATALOGERS. But every morning the headlines would be about the stock market, Panama, or the Middle East. Every afternoon, however, I would get my phone call from the old lady, and every afternoon she would threaten to kill herself.

We were at a standstill. She wouldn't give her name, she wouldn't meet with my catalogers, and she wouldn't be satisfied with the installation of miniblinds. After three weeks of this my nerves were getting frayed.

The next time she called I was ready. I had a strategy — to lie.

"YOUR CATALOGERS ARE PERVERTS!"

"I know. I know."

"YOU DO?" she asked, amazed.

"Yes," I said. "You were right. My catalogers are a bunch of perverts. So I decided to move them to the basement and move my reference librarians up there."

"OH, THANK YOU," she gushed. "THANK YOU. I LOVE REFERENCE LIBRARIANS. THEY ARE SO NICE!"

"Great," I said. "Then you won't call me anymore?"

"No," I won't call you anymore."

I hung up the phone, took a deep breath, and shook my head. "Why are catalogers so misunderstood?" I asked myself. "Why are catalogers so misunderstood?"

Going back to school at the age of forty is a little like going out for the varsity football team at the age of forty. In an effort to deny the obvious deterioration of your body, you tell yourself that you're only as old as you feel and that you're just as adept at playing middle linebacker today as you were when you were eighteen. Fortunately there are rules against forty-year-old men playing intercollegiate football. Too bad that there aren't any rules about forty-year-old men going back to grad school.

I can say that because I made the mistake of seeking a Master's Degree in Public Administration at the age of forty. At the time I didn't think I was making a mistake because, with the exception of math courses, science courses, quantitative research courses, or foreign language courses, I was always a good student in high school, college, and graduate library school. At least I always got my degrees right on schedule. I should have quit, however, while I was ahead.

What exactly possessed me to go back to graduate management school is something I am still not quite sure about, but I think the idea first took shape when I read an article in a library trade journal about how the public library director of the nineties was really more of a public administrator than a librarian. So I decided to go back to school and become a certified public administrator.

I think that I had visions of simply going to a few classes, writing a few short research papers, taking a few exams, and showing up at graduation. That's what age does for you — it clouds your memory. Everybody says that age is a valuable asset because it gives you the wisdom that comes from experience.

Balderdash! The truth is that the older you get the more you forget. You've probably heard the old cliché that "you should enjoy your college years because they are the best years of your life." You never hear young people saying that. People don't start saying that until they turn forty. The closer you are to your college years the more you remember the agonies of final exams, research papers, comprehensives, malevolent professors, foot-long reading lists, tedious textbooks, interminable labs, required courses, and anxiety-filled all night cram sessions. The older you get the more you remember autumn leaves falling on campus, touch football games in the snow, spring break, rush week, toga parties, mud volleyball, and graduation.

Who knows? Maybe I went back to school at the age of forty to recover a lost youth. Maybe I thought that I was still young enough to play mud volleyball. The point is I went back, and five years later I was still there. For five years I tortured myself in pursuit of forty-five credit hours. For five years I sat through four-hour night courses after working eight hours during the day. For five years I got stomachaches over exams and headaches over term papers. For five years I suffered the pangs of high math anxiety in required courses like statistics and quantitative research methods. For five years I dutifully took courses with exciting names like Bureaucracy 507 and read books with fascinating titles like *Changing Organizational Structure: Strategy, Structure, and Professionalism in the United States General Accounting Office.*

But worst of all was the humiliation of being the oldest student in just about every course that I took. I was made to feel like a living historical artifact when during one of our class discussions about the political milieu of the sixties I proudly let slip that I had been in college during the student strike of 1969. One young woman turned around and looked at me with shock. "You're old enough to be my father!" she exclaimed.

At the end of five years, even though I needed only three more credit hours to get my degree, I was convinced that I simply could not continue with the pain and suffering. I was fairly certain that if I had to sit through one more three-hour lecture or take one more test or write one more paper that I would go completely and uncontrollably nuts. You get to a point in life where you have to take a stand and in the immortal words of Roberto Duran say "¡No mas!" I don't care how close to the finish line you are, if your mental or physical health is in jeopardy you must throw in the towel.

"BUT YOU CAN'T JUST QUIT NOW!" my wife told me.

"Yes I can," I said meekly. "Yes I can."

"NO YOU CAN'T. ALL YOU NEED ARE THREE MORE CREDIT HOURS. YOU CANNOT QUIT NOW!"

"I not only can, but I must. My health is at stake. Just thinking about sitting through one more lecture makes my palms sweat profusely, my stomach tighten, my heart pound faster, and my head get dizzy. I CAN'T DO IT! I JUST CAN'T DO IT!"

"THINK OF YOUR CHILDREN, WILL. YOU ARE A ROLE MODEL. YOU CAN'T SET AN EXAMPLE OF QUITTING!"

"I'd rather be a role model of a quitter than a certifiable lunatic."

"IT'S JUST THREE MORE HOURS!"

"READ MY LIPS – I CANNOT DO IT!"

I did it. Under threats of divorce and dismemberment, I sur-
rendered. I signed up for the last three credit hours. "Just think," said
my wife, "when you finish you'll be the library director of the
nineties." But that just didn't seem to motivate me anymore – not
with a course like "Public Sector Labor Relations" in front of me. This
was a required course that I had been putting off for five years. I
couldn't think of anything more boring.

I was even more discouraged when I went to the bookstore to pur-
chase the textbook for the course. It was entitled *Labor Relations in
the Public Sector*, and was written by someone named Richard C.
Kearney. It cost $50 and had a drab olive cover – a boring cover for a
boring book. I am a librarian. In concept, I love all books. But I hated
this book. I hated it from the very first time I saw it. I hated everything
about the book. I hated the cover, I hated the title, I hated the preface,
and I hated the first sentence: "The intent of this initial chapter is to
convey the unique nature of unionization and collective bargaining in
the public sector."

That was as much as I read for fourteen weeks. I went to class, I
took notes, I even wrote a paper, but I could not read the book – not
even the second sentence. I tried to read the book. I really did. Every
Saturday I would sit down at my kitchen table at home. I would
meticulously gather together a notebook, a pen, a neon green text
highlighter, a glass of lemonade, and a bowl of potato chips. Then I
would sit down, open the book, and read the first sentence: "The intent of this initial chapter is to convey the unique nature of unionization and collective bargaining in the public sector."

Then I would get up and go to the bathroom. Then I would check
to see if the morning newspaper had arrived. Then I would check to
see if the mail had arrived. Then I would check the *TV Guide*. Then
I would turn on the television. Then I would watch college football
games all day. Then I would go to bed.

On Sunday morning after returning from church I would sit down
at my kitchen table and meticulously gather together a notebook, a
pen, a neon green text highlighter, a glass of lemonade, and a bowl of
potato chips. Then I would sit down, open the book, and read the first
sentence: "sector. public the in bargaining collective and unionization
of nature unique the convey to is chapter initial this of intent The"

Then I would get up and go to the bathroom. Then I would check to see if the morning newspaper had arrived. Then I would check to see if the mail had arrived and remember it was Sunday. Then I would check the *TV Guide*. Then I would turn on the television. Then I would watch professional football games all day. Then I would go to bed.

This went on for fourteen weeks. At the fifteenth class lecture the professor closed by saying, "Next week is the exam. My advice to all of you would be to study the textbook."

That weekend I resolved to read the entire book, all 359 pages. I was two days away from my degree. All I had to do was stay up for forty-eight hours, read the book, pass the exam, and pick up my diploma. Then the whole nightmare of five and a half years would be finally and mercifully over. I could start my life all over again. "The day after the exam is the first day of the rest of my life," is what I told myself over and over again. It was my mantra.

So on Saturday morning with great resolve I sat down at my kitchen table and gathered together a notebook, a pen, a neon green text highlighter, a glass of lemonade, and a bowl of potato chips. Then I opened the book and read the first sentence: "The of initial is convey unique of and bargaining the sector." intent this chapter to the nature unionization collective in public

Then I got up to go to the bathroom. Then I checked to see if the morning newspaper had arrived. Then I checked to see if the mail had arrived. Then I checked the *TV Guide*. Then I turned on the television set to watch some college football games. But when I turned it on nothing happened. I checked the electric cord. It was plugged in. "LORRAINE!" I called. I was sure she could fix the set. She's good at fixing things.

"Yes, Will?"

"The TV doesn't work."

"I know," she said.

"You do?"

"Yes, I removed a wire from it."

"Why?"

"So that you will read your book."

"Oh."

So I sat down at the kitchen table and opened the book back up. The first sentence had not changed: "The unique intent of public the bargaining is to nature and this collective initial unionization convey in the chapter."

"LORRAINE!" I called out loudly.

"Yes, Will?"

"Lorraine, don't you think the pyracantha out back needs trimming?"

"No, Will, I don't."

"How about the rain gutters. Don't you think I should clean them out this morning?"

"No, Will, I don't."

"In that case, Lorraine, I guess I'll just clean the toilets."

"No, Will."

"BUT YOU DON'T UNDERSTAND, LORRAINE, I WANT TO CLEAN THE TOILETS!"

"Read your book, Will."

Under Lorraine's watchful eye I read and highlighted; read and highlighted; read and highlighted. By Monday morning at 4:00 A.M. I had finished the book. I fell asleep immediately. It was a restless sleep.

Thirteen hours later I walked into class to take the exam — THE LAST EXAM I WOULD EVER TAKE IN MY ENTIRE LIFE. Despite my herculean effort the only thing I could remember from the textbook was the first sentence. I had it memorized. Everything else was a jumble, a chaotic jumble.

But it turned out not to matter. The final exam was one broad conceptual question that I was able to finesse with what I had learned from the class lectures. It was like the textbook never existed.

I am not a book reviewer. It is not my cup of tea. I do not like passing judgment on another person's book, but in the parlance of library trade-journal book reviewers let me say this about *Labor Relations in the Public Sector* by Richard C. Kearney. It is a thoroughly boring book that is not appropriate for small, medium, and large libraries. In fact I wouldn't even recommend it for the Library of Congress.

In summary, it's the kind of book that gives book-burning a good name.

TIME

Ten years ago when I came on board as director of the Tempe Public Library, I walked into a ticklish situation. The library board had just successfully lobbied the City Council for three new professional positions. The city manager, Ken McDonald, a tough old Scotsman, was not pleased. Ken ran a tight ship. He did not believe in adding staff, and he was very upset about the library board's going directly to the City Council. "This must stop," he said to me.

"Yes, Mr. McDonald, but you must remember I was not here when all of this happened. It's not fair to blame me."

"I'm not blaming you. "I'M JUST TELLING YOU NOT TO LET THIS HAPPEN ANYMORE!"

"In my opinion, Mr. McDonald, the library is still understaffed. Tempe has grown dramatically in the past ten years and the library has not kept pace."

"There will be no new staff for at least three more years. No, that's not completely correct. There will be no talk of adding new staff for at least three more years."

"How will we keep up with new business?" I asked.

"With volunteers," he said definitively. "In my opinion most of the work in a library can be done with volunteers."

"But, sir," I persisted, "very few volunteers have the necessary training."

"Will, I don't want to hear anything more about this. If you need more staff you go out and get volunteers or you go out and get yourself another job."

"Yes, sir."

At the time I was insulted. Mr. McDonald, like many other people, obviously did not have a great deal of respect for the skills, talents, and abilities of people who work in libraries. He obviously felt that you could take anyone off the street and make a librarian out of him. For three weeks I sulked.

But then realizing that sulking wasn't going to help with the problem at hand, I called a woman named Carol Shannon into my office. Carol was a pleasant person who had worked at the library for many years in a wide variety of jobs. In my opinion she knew the library and the community as well as anyone on staff. I had confidence in her. What I liked best about her was that she always told me what I needed to hear; not what I wanted to know.

"Carol, we need to start a volunteer program."

"What brought this on?"

"Mr. McDonald won't hear of any new staff requests. He thinks volunteers are the answer. We have to at least give his idea a shot. Then when it doesn't work we can ask him for more staff."

"Will, I think it will work. I think Mr. McDonald is right. I myself am a volunteer at the hospital. There are a lot of good people out there."

"Okay, Carol, come back to me in a week with your ideas."

Carol came back with a plan. She said that the one area of the library where the regular staff had the greatest need for additional help was in periodicals — organizing the collection, retrieving magazines for patrons, and putting them away. In her words, "You do not need a Ph.D. or an M.L.S. to work in periodicals."

"Okay," I said skeptically, "start recruiting people and put them to work."

Within a month, Carol's fledging volunteer program was up and running. I had to hand it to her. She had attracted some very good, conscientious workers. Most of them were older, retired people who possessed a good old-fashioned work ethic. I was both surprised and pleased. The program was proving to be a big hit with the staff and the public. Mr. McDonald couldn't have been happier. "I'm very pleased with the job you're doing, Will."

There was only one volunteer of whom I was skeptical. He was a younger man who gave the appearance of shiftlessness. His name was Jerry. Jerry had longish, unkempt hair, and he wore baggy, ill-fitting clothes. He did not exactly project the image that you want for your library, but Carol really liked him. "He's helpful, personable, responsible, and very intelligent," she said.

"If he's so intelligent," I said, "why doesn't he get a real job?"

"I really don't know what his situation is. He doesn't like to talk about himself."

"He's probably hiding something," I said. "If you ask me, this guy could be trouble."

"I think you're wrong," said Carol firmly.

I decided to find out for myself. Whenever I noticed that Jerry was on duty I would stop by and chat with him. Carol was right. He was personable, helpful, and very intelligent. He told me that he had a college degree, and I believed him. He was very articulate in his shy and modest way. I decided he wasn't a bad guy, just lazy — a hippie from the sixties who didn't want to despoil his personal virtue by making a living in our capitalistic society. I hated to see him waste his life.

Months went by and Jerry became a regular part of the ebb and flow of everyday life in our library. And then the rumors started. Jerry was supposedly an ice cream magnate. This long-haired, rag-tag volunteer was a big wheel in the ice cream industry, a real innovator. I scoffed at the rumors—"And my name is Donald Trump."

Eventually the scuttlebutt became more specific. Carol told me that Jerry had started a Vermont ice cream company that had tremendous growth potential. I ended that speculation with one quick question, "Then what's he doing in Arizona?"

That was a question no one could really answer. Soon the rumors died and Jerry went from being Jerry the Ice Cream Magnate back to Jerry the Hippie. But this didn't last long. Another rumor started. Supposedly, Jerry was taking a break from the ice cream industry. His girlfriend was in graduate school at Arizona State and he had come to Tempe to be with her.

"You just don't take a break from your company," I said sardonically. "I'm telling you Jerry is a nice, harmless, lazy hippie. He'll never amount to a hill of beans. Don't get me wrong, I like Jerry, but he's no venture capitalist."

Two weeks later a magazine article about ice cream appeared mysteriously on my desk. It was from the August 10, 1981, edition of *Time*. The first sentence of the article was "What you must understand at the outset is that Ben and Jerry's, in Burlington, Vermont, makes the best ice cream in the world." A few pages later there was a picture of Ben Cohen and Jerry Greenfield, the makers of the best ice cream in the world. No doubt about it, Jerry Greenfield was in fact Jerry, the volunteer.

"Big deal," I said to the library staffer who had left the article on my desk. "So Ben and Jerry put out an expensive superpremium ice cream that happens to be the latest yuppie fad. It will pass."

My curiosity, however, was piqued, and I made it a point to bump into Jerry that day. "Jerry," I said, "I saw your picture in *Time* magazine. Congratulations. Your ice cream must be pretty good. It's too bad you can only get it in New England."

"Thank you," he said modestly, "but right now Ben is running the show. I'm kind of on the outside."

A few weeks later Jerry left Tempe and returned to Vermont. We didn't really hear much about Jerry for some time, and then all of a sudden you couldn't turn on the television or open a magazine without seeing the face of Jerry Greenfield. If he wasn't bringing ice cream to the Soviet Union, he was saving the rain forest or helping with farm aid or waging legal battles against a large corporation that was trying to keep his ice cream off grocery store shelves. Jerry was all over the place.

"Pretty lazy guy, right Will?" said Carol.

"Big deal," I said. "The liberal press has found its darling. You wait. In six months, Jerry and his ice cream will be as out of fashion as the Nehru jacket."

That was three years ago. Since then Jerry and his company has become hotter than ever (annual sales of $50 million), and his ice cream has even reached Arizona. I discovered that last fact by accident. My wife and kids and I were in a Scottsdale bookstore doing some Christmas shopping when I overheard two people talking about an incredible new ice cream shop that had opened next door. One of them said, "It carries a new ice cream called Ben and Jerry's that is like nothing you've ever tasted. It's heaven."

At that point I felt compelled to enter into the conversation. "I must correct you," I said. "Ben and Jerry's ice cream is not new. It's been around for ten years. We're just getting an opportunity to experience it out here in Arizona."

"How did you happen to know about it?" the other shopper asked.

"Hey," I said with a big, proud smile. "Jerry Greenfield and I go way back. In fact, he used to work for me. He volunteered at my library."

"He did?"

"Yes, and I always knew that boy was going to be a big success."

There was no other alternative. I had to take a vacation. For seven years I had not taken a vacation. This wasn't because I couldn't find the time or didn't have the money. The truth is I am philosophically opposed to vacations.

This has something to do with my childhood. My parents were vacationgoers. Every summer for eighteen years they dragged me and my brother and sister from motel to motel on the way to Florida, New England, the Great Smoky Mountains, the Adirondacks, the Trapp Family Lodge, the Catskills, the Paul Revere House, the Eastern Shore, the streets of Savannah, the Finger Lakes, Fort Ticonderoga, Davy Crockett's log cabin, Lake George, the White Mountains, Prince Edward Island, the Bay of Fundy, the sands of Nova Scotia, Monticello, Mount Vernon, the Shenandoah Mountains, and yes, even something in Georgia called the Dismal Swamp. If there was a mountain range, lake, or historic house between Newfoundland and Daytona Beach that we missed I would be sincerely surprised.

Today, many years later, these vacation destinations loom like battlefields in my mind. Each one was attained only after a considerable struggle that included carsickness, flat tires, being poked by my brother in the backseat, overheated radiators, fights over where to eat dinner, faulty electrical systems, carsickness, flat tires, errant short cuts, dipsy doodle roads, fights over where to eat lunch, carsickness, flat tires, chuckholes, getting lost, overheated radiators, blown carburetors, being poked by my sister in the backseat and fights over what motel to stop at for the night.

Ah, the motels — they were the best part of the trips. First, there was the ordeal of the selection. My mother, not totally trusting her AAA, Duncan Hines, and Mobil Travel guides, would always insist on inspecting the bathrooms. If the bathrooms were clean, we stayed; if they were the least bit dusty, we moved on down the road. Sometimes it took three or four stops before we found the right one.

Then the fun would begin — bouncing on the bed, splashing in the pool, dropping coins in the vending machine, trying out the bed vibrator, and turning up the TV to full blast. That may not sound like a lot of fun, but compared to being squeezed into the back of the car for eight to ten hours a day, it was heaven.

When I think of those vacations now, I think of a blur. Most of the sights that we supposedly "visited" were seen at 75 mph. "See that hole in the ground," my father would say, "that is the Carlsbad

Caverns. Take a good look at it because I'm not going to stop. I'm just going to slow down." Five minutes later we would be back on the highway doing 75 mph. That was the speed limit in those days. There was no energy crisis and our interstate highway system had not yet deteriorated.

Early each morning my father would pack us into the car (we progressed over the years from a '57 Mercury to a '61 Rambler station wagon to a '65 Pontiac sedan) and then hurry us out onto the nearest interstate. With Dad at the wheel and our destination targets marked systematically on a roadmap mounted on the dashboard, our car, like a rocket ship pointed at the moon, would rarely veer off course.

But then after five or six hours, my father, who was now at the point of exhaustion, would turn the wheel over to Mom and fall fast asleep in the passenger's seat. Where Dad was strictly an interstate type of guy, Mom loved to explore the back roads. "There's a scenic view we should see on the other side of that mountain," she would say. Then with great enthusiasm, she would exit the interstate and try, usually unsuccessfully, to navigate us through an unfamiliar web of secondary roads to the place on the map that had caught her fancy. My father, of course, would wake up in horror to see that we were now behind schedule and traveling 35 mph on a curvy one lane road. It did not make for a happy time.

These vacations seemed to dramatize my parents' differences. My mother, a Latin and French teacher, was a humanist. My father, on the other hand, was a scientist. For fifty weeks of the year their personalities seemed more complimentary than contrasting. In fact, I felt that as a child I had the best of both worlds. What my father could not offer in the way of warmth, sympathy, and intuition was provided in abundance by my mother. What she could not give in terms of logic, reason, and sound judgment was offered in plentitude by my father. When I need a tear wiped I went to my mother; when I needed a problem solved my Dad was always there to help me.

Except on vacations. On vacations our family compatibility sputtered and broke down almost as often as our cars overheated and malfunctioned. I wonder how many families crash and burn every summer on the highways and byways of Vacationland, U.S.A. To this day I am inordinately thankful that somehow our own sense of family togetherness is still intact in spite of our eighteen years of summertime trips.

What a relief it was finally, after two seemingly interminable weeks of travel, to get back home from someplace like the Adirondack Mountains or the Dismal Swamp. What a pleasure to crawl into your own bed secure in the knowledge that tomorrow you wouldn't be throwing up in the backseat of a car. If there was one positive thing about all those vacations, it was that they made me appreciate the modest pleasures of my everyday routine at home.

Home was where everyone in my family had his or her own special niche. I realize now that those vacations were dangerous because they pulled us out of our comfortable little niches and thrust us into an atmosphere of freedom that we were not prepared to handle. Suddenly we had to make decisions that for fifty weeks of the year were determined by our individual daily routines and responsibilities. It is within this context of uncertainty that individual differences can surface and fester.

That is why I have never taken my own kids on a vacation. "Why can't we be like other families," they will ask, "and take trips to Disneyland or the Grand Canyon?"

"Because we can't!" is how I always answer. And then by way of explanation I always point out to them that the Nintendo set that I gave them for Christmas was intended to be their summer vacation.

For many, many years I avoided taking a vacation. But then suddenly this pattern changed when my wife decided that she wanted to pay a surprise visit to her father back in Indiana on his birthday. "You will have to take a week of vacation and stay home with the kids while I am gone," she said.

Actually this didn't sound bad. This would be a vacation but it certainly wouldn't be one spent on an interstate highway and my wife wouldn't be at home in her usual role of supervisor of home, yard, and garage maintenance. In other words I wouldn't be washing windows, cleaning out rain gutters, sweeping floors, or trimming bushes under her critical eye.

I pictured a week of leisurely breakfasts, afternoon catnaps, and dinners of home-delivered anchovy pizzas. I was determined not to leave the friendly confines of my bedroom, my family room, and my backyard. For all I cared, my three boys could do nothing but play Nintendo games and watch television. I hadn't had a week off in years and I was determined to do nothing but vegetate. In my mind I felt completely deserving of this quality leisure time opportunity.

My staff wholeheartedly agreed. "Will, you certainly deserve to take it easy for awhile. In fact you ought to do this more often," is what everybody at the library told me when I announced my vacation plans. I found out a few hours later, however, that the staff really felt that they were the ones who deserved to get me out of the library for a week. I was down in the fiction trying to select some good books to vegetate with during my week of leisure when I overheard two reference librarians talking about me.

"Can you believe that Manley is actually going to take some time off. I never thought I'd see the day."

"I won't believe it until I see it."

"Imagine coming to work in the morning and not having to worry about him descending out of his office and looking over your shoulder while you're answering a reference question."

"Imagine not having to listen to his lectures about when he was a reference librarian in the days before they had computers."

"Yeah, it's going to be absolute heaven around here for a whole week."

For a second, for a brief second, I considered canceling my vacation plans out of spite. But I came to my senses when I refocused my mind's eye on the prospect of lying out in the sun with a good book and a cold mug of root beer.

On Sunday evening I put my wife on the plane. Right up until the time they took her ticket she filled the air with motherly advice: "Don't give the kids peanut butter all week! Don't let them watch *Married . . . With Children*! And, above all, don't let Stephen play Nintendo more than an hour and a half a day!" As soon as her plane took off I chuckled about how much fun the kids were going to have eating peanut butter, watching television, and playing Nintendo.

The joke, it turned out, was on me. The next morning the boys woke me up at 7:00. "Time to get up, Dad—batting practice starts in a half hour!"

"What?"

"Batting practice starts in a half hour. Then it's fielding practice and the game. We'll take a short break for lunch, and then play the second game of our doubleheader after lunch."

"What are you talking about?"

"Mom's not here, Dad. We can play baseball all week."

"But guys this is Arizona in August. It's too hot to play baseball."

"Don't be a weenie."

"Come on, guys, let me sleep."

"Sorry, Dad." Suddenly three boys were pulling me out of bed.

A half hour later I was pitching batting practice on a very hot elementary school playground to my three boys. We played for four hours before they would let me take them home for lunch. Forty-five minutes after lunch, I was pitching the second half of a doubleheader. On one particular pitch I felt a muscle rip in my right leg. The pain was excruciating. I gave out a loud groan. "Suck it up, Dad," is what my guys said to me in sympathy.

"No, you guys don't understand," I said. "I need to see a doctor. I am in intense pain."

"Dad, the pros play in pain!"

"Guys, I can't go on."

"Dad, you have to play. We only have six and a half days of vacation left. We were planning on playing baseball all week. Please don't let us down. You don't want us to hate you for the rest of our lives, do you?"

I struggled on for three more hours. Finally, I said, "That's it! That's enough for today." When I got home, I hobbled over to the phone which was ringing. It was one of my employees.

"Will, we need your evaluation file. Where is it?"

"Oh," I said suddenly seeing an opportunity to escape my boys, "I'm not really sure where I put it but I'll be glad to come down to the library and find it for you."

"No, that's not necessary. We'll wait until you get back."

"Look," I said, "tell everyone that if they need me for even the slightest thing I would be more than happy to come on over. In fact, I'd even be willing to cut back on my vacation just to help out."

"No, everything is fine, Will. Relax and enjoy yourself."

"But you don't understand. I don't mind being bothered," I said while rubbing my leg. "Don't be afraid to call."

"Right now everything is fine, Will."

"Don't you get it?" I finally siad. "I WANT TO COME BACK! MY KIDS ARE DRIVING ME CRAZY! PLEASE CALL ME TOMORROW MORNING AND TELL ME THERE IS A CRISIS!"

No one ever called.

But that's all right. I know how to get revenge on my staff. I'll just never take another vacation in my life.

The thing about working for a board of trustees is that there are so many of them. The average American working stiff has one boss, and one boss only. Admittedly that boss can sometimes be a pain but still there's only one of him or her.

The average American library director, however, works for five, seven, nine, and sometimes as many as fifteen bosses. A "multiheaded monster" is how one of my colleagues refers to his library board. While none of the boards that I've worked for could ever be considered even remotely monstrous, their sheer size always kept me on my toes. Keeping nine bosses happy all at the same time is a very challenging balancing act that ranks right up there with tightrope walking and sword juggling—or, perhaps more accurately, sword juggling while tightrope walking.

In the workaday world, rule number one will always and forever be: GET ALONG WITH YOUR BOSS. If you can't get along with your boss two things will happen: you will end up being very miserable, and you will end up being very unemployed.

Getting along with the boss is an art form. Success, more often than not, depends on what you don't do rather than what you do. For instance, it should be commonsensical that you should not call your boss a jerk to his face. And yet I have seen people, who have obviously watched too many Clint Eastwood movies, do just that. They become unemployed very quickly.

Once you have mastered the art of not calling your boss a jerk, you next need to learn your boss's idiosyncrasies. By my calculations every boss has four. For instance, my first boss was never civil before noon; he hated men who wore paisley ties; he detested Christmas; and he enjoyed smoking cigars. Other than that he was a fully integrated, well adjusted human being. As long as you did your job, didn't call him a jerk, didn't try to talk to him before noon, didn't wear paisley ties, didn't wish him a Merry Christmas, and didn't inform him of the carcinogenic effect of secondary cigar smoke, he would never bother you.

There is, however, an important distinction between your boss never bothering you and your boss actually liking you. To get your boss to like you, you have to become proactive. You have to actively attempt to do and say all the right things. Just staying out of trouble will not do the job.

The first thing you have to do is identify what the boss believes in. Most bosses have three strong beliefs, usually in the areas of religion, politics, and sports. For instance, if your boss is a Roman Catholic Democrat who loves the Chicago Cubs it would be very intelligent of you to (a) convert to Catholicism, (b) say some derogatory things about lame-brained Republicans, and (c) start wearing a Cubs hat. Sooner than you think, your value in the eyes of the boss will go up immeasureably.

But don't get cocky. If you really want to endear yourself to your boss you need to endear yourself to your boss's spouse, because, let's face it, the boss's spouse is often the boss's boss. Taking the boss's spouse lightly can be fatal. I know of one book collection developer who refused to order a book that his boss's spouse recommended.

"When do you expect my book to come in from the publisher?" asked the boss's spouse after three weeks of waiting.

"I decided not to order it."

"YOU WHAT?"

"I decided not to order it. Our policy is that a new novel must have two positive reviews before we can order it. The one you suggested unfortunately didn't even get one."

"WE'LL SEE ABOUT THAT!"

Two days later the book collection developer was told to check out the job announcements in *Library Journal*, dust off his résumé, and take his talents elsewhere. When I asked him why he didn't fight his dismissal he said that it didn't take him long to realize that even if he were able to keep his job he didn't relish the prospect of being proactively disliked by his boss's spouse on a long term basis. "She's just too unrelenting," he confided.

The lesson in all of this, of course, is that for the boss's spouse you break the rules. You do what you have to do because it's an unavoidable fact of life that for better or worse till death or divorce drive them apart, the boss has to live with his spouse. If the spouse doesn't like one of the boss's employees, the boss will hear about it at breakfast, lunch, dinner, and bedtime. To preserve domestic tranquility, enhance mental stability, and save the marriage, it's a sure bet that the boss will unload the targeted employee. In many respects, therefore, it is more important to get along with the boss's spouse than with the boss.

I know of one children's librarian who uses an "out of sight/out of mind" strategy. Whenever she sees the boss's spouse coming she just disappears. "I don't want the spouse to even know I'm alive," is how she puts it.

This is a nice approach if you can get away with it. Frequently, however, it's not very realistic. Library organizations have too many parties, dinners, and miscellaneous social events that you are expected to attend, and the boss's spouse is always there to inspect the troops. So what you have to do is exhaustively research the spouse's idiosyncrasies, values, and opinions, and always keep them in mind whenever the spouse happens to be around. Getting along with the spouse, therefore, is certainly problematic but by no means impossible. It's really a matter of keeping a low profile, avoiding idiosyncratic minefields, and saying the right things at the right time.

It's also a matter of not saying the wrong things at the wrong time. Very simply, you should never, ever, criticize the boss's spouse to anyone. For some reason library grapevines lead right to the spouse. How? I don't know, but I am familiar with a situation in which a reference librarian mumbled something under his breath about the boss's spouse that rhymed with the word "witch." Two days later that little epithet got back to the spouse, and two days after that our reference librarian found himself down in the periodicals room to do fetch and carry work for the rest of his life. So deep was he in the boss's doghouse that we began calling him Rover and leaving dog biscuits in his in-basket.

Getting along with your boss is like any other relationship — you really have to work at it. If you're thoughtful, considerate, and halfway intelligent you should have pretty clear sailing. Getting along with your board of trustees, however, is a different matter. Here the variables multiply very rapidly. The average library board has nine trustees. These nine trustees are usually all married. That means that you have nine bosses and nine spouses to endear yourself to. If you accept my rule of thumb that everyone has at least four idiosyncrasies and three strong beliefs, that means that you have to master and deal with seventy-two idiosyncrasies and fifty-four strong beliefs.

But that's not all. You very rarely have an opportunity to deal with one of your trustees on an individual basis. You usually have to deal with them collectively, and that is a much more complex challenge because of something called chemistry. Everything I know about chemistry I learned in my freshman year of high school when my teacher mixed sodium and water together and the resulting sparks burned a hole in my shirt and in my face.

That's sort of what happens when library trustees get together. Sometimes sparks fly and sometimes you get burned. So right from the start you have to learn two things: how to keep the sparks from flying, and how to stay out of the way when you can't keep the sparks from flying. The following represents all of my unprofessional advice on how to do that.

1. NEVER WEAR A CUBS HAT

NEVER play up to the idiosyncrasies and strong beliefs of any one trustee on your board. For instance, even if you find out that the president of your board is a Cubs fanatic, never wear a Cubs hat to try to please or impress him because there is a very good chance that there is someone else on the board who hates the Cubs. Likewise, never, even in informal moments, succumb to the temptation of saying anything remotely related to religion, sex, politics, and money. If you do, you're sure to offend someone. For example, I made the mistake in front of my entire board of referring to Evan Mecham (the Arizona governor who was impeached and removed from office in 1988) as a "no good racist Nazi." This man Mecham was such a bad governor that I couldn't imagine anyone having any respect for him. Unfortunately, as soon as I said that one of my trustees indicated to me (not very politely) that he had served on Mecham's campaign committee and thought the world of him. Fortunately for me, this trustee's term expired in three weeks. Otherwise my term might have been expiring.

2. SWITZERLAND IS THE MOST BEAUTIFUL COUNTRY IN THE WORLD

Never allow yourself to get pulled into the undertow of board alliances and cliques. Every board has them, and from time to time you will feel strong pressure to get involved. Resist this pressure! Alliances are tricky creatures. They can change colors very quickly, leaving you high, dry, and unemployed. Whenever a trustee wants you to take his side in an internal board dispute just think of neutral Switzerland. It's the most beautiful country in the world.

3. WE ARE FAMILY

There can be a great temptation from time to time to mumble something disparaging about a trustee who has done or said something significantly stupid. For instance, I once had a trustee who wanted me to tear apart the entire east wall of our library and install drive up windows so that people could pick up their books from their cars as if the library were a fast food emporium. There was a great temptation for me to dismiss this idea as "the stupidest thing I had ever heard of" but I had to bite my tongue and methodically explain why a public library cannot function like a Burger King.

If I had said something derogatory, I would not only have offended the trustee with the stupid idea but the entire board as well. Never forget that despite their differences, the trustees on a board function as a kind of family, and it's a family that you, the hired hand, are not a part of. It's the old adage that I can call my brother a jerk but the minute you call him a jerk you better be ready to fight me.

4. DON'T HIRE A TRUSTEE'S DAUGHTER

One of the worst things you can do is break policy and give a special favor to one board member. If, for example, you hire one trustee's daughter to work as a page be prepared to hire everyone's daughter, and if you don't have enough money in your budget, be prepared to get the necessary dollars and cents out of your own salary.

Trustees can get very jealous of each other over very, very little things. That was one of the first board lessons I ever learned. I had a trustee who was normally very nice to me, but for a three-week period he became very unfriendly, almost belligerent. Finally I worked up the courage to ask him what was wrong. "I'm very bitter," he said, "that you allowed Don Tarleton [a fellow trustee] to take the new Stephen King book even though I asked for it first." I was shocked for two reasons. First, I couldn't believe that such a trivial matter could cause such deep resentment, and second, I never gave Tarleton the book. He took it out of the cataloging room without staff's knowledge. But this trustee was convinced that I had done Tarleton a special favor. Fortunately I didn't lose my job over this crisis, but it was nip and tuck for a while.

5. *STAY OUT OF THE KITCHEN*

For many of the issues that come before the board, especially in the area of library policies, it is both appropriate and important for the library director to offer the benefit of his or her professional knowledge and experience. There are other issues, however, that directors should stay twenty miles away from. Planning menus for board dinners, get-togethers, social events, and receptions is one of those areas. Library directors have no business offering advice about food. I know. I learned the hard way.

I had been the library director for all of two weeks when my board started discussing the annual trustee banquet. As was their custom, the trustees wanted to plan a lavish event in an expensive local restaurant. When they started talking about open bars and prime rib I just couldn't contain myself. I had to offer my unprofessional opinions.

"By my calculations the kind of event that you are planning will cost over a thousand dollars."

"Yes," said the chair of the social committee, "that's about right. Last year we were in that neighborhood."

"But don't you think the money could be better used to buy books? After all, it is public money."

There was a silence, a long, very uncomfortable silence. Silences bother me greatly so I started talking again. "If you want to have a dinner, there are a lot of nice things on the menu that cost a lot less than prime rib."

Again there was silence, this time a kind of aggressive silence, one that challenged me to open my mouth again. I took the challenge. "I mean, I don't even like prime rib."

By now the president of the board was standing. "I think," he said emphatically, "that we should take a recess for five minutes." Then he looked at me and said, "Will, step into the kitchen for a minute."

The kitchen was adjacent to the board room and I sidled nervously over to the refrigerator. "Will, in the two weeks you've been here, you've done a very nice job. The staff seems to like you and the community seems to like you. But if you want your tenure to last more than two weeks, I have a suggestion."

"Please, what is it?" I asked anxiously.

"LET THE BOARD PLAN ITS OWN MENUS!"

I nodded my head sheepishly and started to walk back to the board room. But before I could get out of the kitchen my board president called me back. "Now, Will, before you go back to the board table I want to know one thing."

"What?"

"How do you like prime rib?"

"I love it."

"Good."

DOMESTIC VIOLENCE

Yesterday, after reflecting on the six-month insurance premium of $588 for my '82 Chevette (we have a teenage driver in the family), I made what I thought was a rather startling pronouncement to my family at the dinner table. "I hate automobiles!"

No one, however, seemed to be paying attention. My three sons were busy attacking their corn on the cob and my wife's attention seemed to be fastened on a bird pecking away at a piece of suet that was in the feeder outside our window. "I don't think anyone heard me, but I happen to hate automobiles."

Finally my son Stephen looked up at me, yawned, and then nonchalantly said, "Then why do you drive one?"

"To get around," I quickly countered. "But that doesn't mean I can't hate automobiles. They are expensive, they waste energy, they pollute the environment, they kill and maim thousands of people every year, and they distort personal values."

"Well," said Stephen, "I can't wait until I get my driver's license. You know what I hate?"

"What?" asked my wife.

"I hate August."

"Why?" I asked.

"Because it is hot, because there are no holidays in August, and because we go back to school in August."

Next up was Michael, my youngest son. "You know what I hate?" he asked.

"What?" we all inquired.

"I hate other people's birthdays. I wish everybody's birthday was my own!"

"That's selfish," said Stephen. "I happen to like my birthday."

"You know what I hate?" said David.

"No," we all said at once. David is the oldesst and he rarely talks at dinner.

"I hate red meat." We were all eating red meat.

"Why?" I asked, confused. Red meat is one of the things that salvages life for me.

"Because it has negative nutritional value," he answered.

"Well, that may be," I said, "but as you get older you will see that life is not easy. A good steak helps ease the pain."

"Speaking of pain," said my wife, "I hate overdue fines. I hate overdue fines more than anything in the world. Do you know what this family pays in overdue fines per year. I'd hate to even total it up. It's too depressing. Today we got a greedy little letter from the library saying we now owe twenty dollars. Where does it stop?"

"I hate overdues too," said Stephen. David and Michael instantly agreed with him. They also hated library fines. Then everyone looked up at me as if I were the devil incarnate — the man responsible for the overdue fine.

"Now wait a minute, everybody," I said. "I didn't invent library fines. I happen to hate them also. I hate them because they are not effective as a deterrent. I'm a prime example. Even though I've paid hundreds, who knows, maybe even thousands of dollars in fines, I still routinely return my books late. I hate them because people think that libraries are totally funded by fines. I hate them because they give libraries and librarians a bad name. No, don't put this on me. I didn't invent fines!"

Well, then who did invent them?" asked Michael curiously.

"That," I said to Michael, "is a very fascinating question. In all my studies and in all my work I have never heard anyone raise that question before. I guess we all assume that library fines are like the birds and the trees — God made them in that first week of creation."

"So what you're saying," said Stephen with a smirk, "is that fines have a divine origin."

"Yeah, blame it on God," I said, happy to have the burden off my shoulders.

As is the case with most dinner conversations this one broke up rather quickly as the five of us went off in our own directions. But the question of who invented the library fine is something that stuck with me like a leaf caught in the cuff of my pants. It was an interesting question. Who exactly was it who had originated the idea of the fine? What kind of a person had shackled the library profession with the onerous task of inflicting this unfortunate form of punishment on literally millions of readers? What manner of neurosis would such a person suffer from, that it would impel him to penalize people for taking too long to read a book? Would he want to fine his doctor if he took too long to perform a heart surgery?

It had to be one of two types of people: one of those hoary old pompous founding fathers like Charles Ammi Cutter, Ainsworth Rand Spofford, or the inimitable John Cotton Dana, or one of those stereotypical library harpies like Gertrude Mustard Strong who had been the first to perfect the fine art of driving people right out of the library with one beady-eyed stare. But then again maybe there wasn't any one specific villain on whom you could pin the blame.

I went to my library science collection to find out. First, I started with reference books, specifically *The ALA World Encyclopedia of Library and Information Services.* This grandiose compendium of library history, however, does not deign to mention the humble fine. It is obviously above that sort of thing. So next I checked the circulating collection and leafed through an impressive array of boring books with titles like *Introduction to American Library Thought.* Again I could find no mention of the lowly overdue fine.

This was outrageous. There was plenty in these books about cataloging, clay tablets, intellectual freedom, and added entries but nothing, I repeat, nothing, on the subject of fines, let alone on the subject of who invented the blasted things. This was preposterous. Nothing is more strongly associated with libraries than the overdue fine. Were our profession's most noble authors trying to create the impression that overdue fines do not exist? That they are only a figment of our demented public's imagination? This was like opening a history of World War II and finding no mention of the Holocaust.

And then it hit me—the reference classic *Famous First Facts* would certainly have a listing for the first library fine. In my reference days this book had gotten me out of many a pickle. I quickly grabbed it off the shelf and turned to the word "library"—first library bookwagon, first business library supported by taxes, first children's library, first library catalog, and first library society. Where was the first library fine? It was not there. This was ridiculous. How could you list the first library bookwagon and not the first library fine? This was getting spooky.

My reveries, however, were interrupted by a phone call. It was my secretary. "Will, there is a man here to see you. He says he has an appointment."

"I don't remember an appointment."

"Well, he's here and he's not going away."

"I'll be right up."

The man who was waiting to see me was a salesman. I could have guessed that. Most salesman never make an appointment, but when they show up at your office they pretend that they have not only made an appointment but that they are upset with you for forgetting about it. They want you to feel guilty so that you will buy whatever they are selling.

"Mr. Manley, I am here to represent the West Brook Bill Collection Agency. We are a small but aggressive agency that I think can be of great help to your library."

"Oh, in what way?" I asked with great curiosity. I couldn't imagine any use for a collection agency.

"For your overdue problem!"

"Our overdue problem?"

"Yes, I've talked to your circulation people and I understand that almost 20 percent of the books that are checked out of your library are overdue."

"They are?"

"Yes, and now you can do something about it."

"I can?"

"Yes, our agency has an excellent track record for collecting overdue fines. First we send a letter to the offender. In 80 percent of the cases this does the trick. When it doesn't work we call the delinquent borrowers, and when that doesn't work we send a guard out to the person's home."

"A guard? You mean a man in a uniform like at the mall?"

"Yes, and our guards, unlike the ones at the mall, are fully armed. You'd be surprised how hostile some of these delinquent borrowers can get when our guards show up requesting fine monies."

"Oh, I can imagine. I for one would get very hostile myself."

"Do you think that you would be interested in contracting with our company for a ninety-day trial period?"

"No, I don't think this is our style here in Tempe. I'm really not interested in your service."

"What?" Don't you think we can do the job?"

"Yes, I'm sure you can."

"Then what's wrong?"

My family owes twenty dollars. I wouldn't want a homicide to occur in my home when your armed guard shows up to collect."

"Don't you worry about your family, Mr. Manley. Our guards very rarely have to get tough with anyone."

"Oh, it's not my family I'm worried about, it's your guard. I wouldn't be able to guarantee his safety in my household. We tend to be very violent about the matter of fines."

Nutritionists say, "You are what you eat." Designers say, "You are what you wear." English teachers say, "You are what you read." Car salesmen say, "You are what you drive." And real estate agents say, "You are what you live in." But none of this is true. Not really. The real truth is, "You are what you are." What you are is what you do, as in what you do for a living.

Whether we like it or not, others define and judge us by our profession or occupation. When the person sitting next to you on an airplane asks, "What are you?" you don't say, "I am a father of three sons, a Roman Catholic, a lover of chocolate, and a fan of the Philadelphia Phillies." You say, "I am a librarian." And then all of a sudden that person who has known you less than fifteen seconds begins to make definite conclusions about your character and personality. He or she begins to connect you personally to all the stereotypes there are about librarians.

Although we librarians protest incessantly about these stereotypes, the truth is that there is not a profession or occupation that does not suffer from stereotypes. Accountants are boring. Lawyers are devious. Politicians are crooks. Bankers are heartless. Plumbers are boorish. Used car salesman are liars. The list does not stop.

We librarians, of course, are stereotyped as humorless, bookish, and boring. Although benign, this image is not terribly endearing. That may be one of the reasons why I have never met anyone who grew up always wanting to be a librarian. "It sort of just happened" is how most people describe their initiation into the library profession.

More often than not librarianship represents a second, third, or fourth career choice. "I didn't have the time, money, or stamina to pursue a Ph.D. in my undergraduate major so I went to library school," is a statement you often hear from librarians when they talk about the genesis of their careers. "I didn't want to teach, but I liked the academic environment. Library science seemed like the perfect alternative," is another remark you often hear. But I have also seen many librarians, especially those who have been in the field for quite some time, give a panicked look of confusion when asked why or how they got into the profession. "How DID I get into this field?" is a question you can see them asking themselves.

If someone had told me while I was growing up that I would become a librarian I would have, depending upon my mood, either laughed at the person or punched him out. My lot in life was to be a professional athlete. I pictured myself as a sort of Renaissance man for all sports seasons. I would be second baseman for the Philadelphia Phillies, defensive back for the Green Bay Packers, and point guard for the New York Knicks. In my spare time I would train for the Olympic mile. Until I was thirteen it never occurred to me that my future might not materialize exactly as I had envisioned it. And even then I still fully expected to become second baseman for the Phillies. It was the football and basketball career that I had my doubts about.

By the end of my senior year in high school, however, the harsh truth began to emerge. Although I had made the All–South Jersey baseball team, no major league club had offered me so much as a try-out. I could hit and field well enough but my throwing arm, I was told, was of the powder-puff variety—definitely not big league quality.

This forced me to re-evaluate my career plans. Since I could not be a professional baseball player, I decided it might be nice to be a United States senator. I came to this conclusion by a process of elimination. After stumbling badly through every science, math, shop, and art class that I had ever taken, I realized that I would never be a doctor, engineer, architect, or accountant. That left law or educa-tion. Since I didn't have the least interest in becoming a lawyer or teacher, I decided that my only alternative was to become a United States senator.

Three months later, in September of 1967 I entered college. Up until 1967 college had always been seen (and is seen today) as an oc-cupational preparatory school. "Go to college so you can get a good job," was the conventional wisdom on the lips of every counselor, teacher, parent, or community leader. But in the late sixties, colleges and universities from Boston to Berkeley had become centers of poliical activism fighting war, poverty, racism, pollution, and the military-industrial complex. The purpose of higher education was no longer to produce highly qualified applicants for high paying jobs but rather to develop highly educated men and women committed to sav-ing the world.

This was a time of war, and Selma, Kent State, Watts, and Saigon are names that have become symbolic of the battlegrounds on which the skirmishes of the sixties were fought. Getting a good job was not nearly as important as staying alive, and the key to staying alive was putting an end to the hostilities in Vietnam. War protest, therefore, became an art form. Interestingly enough, many of our protests were aimed at the very employers—Dow Chemical, the F.B.I. and the C.I.A.—that college students had traditionally welcomed with open arms. For instance, when Dow Chemical Company (manufacturer of napalm) came to my school (Notre Dame) to recruit job candidates, we set up a human wall of bodies in front of the room where they intended to conduct interviews. At the time it seemed to me that we were not only protesting the Vietnam War, we were also protesting the regimentation of the workaday world. Above all else, freedom and nonconformity were valued in the 1960s, and these were qualities that were antithetical to getting a job and making a living.

Eventually, however, as the war in Vietnam wound down, it became obvious that being a war protestor was an occupation with a limited future. That, of course, meant that finding a job became a higher priority. Since there were no openings for the position of senator in my home state of New Jersey, I was totally at a loss as to what I wanted to do with my liberal arts education. The thought happened to occur to me that I would like to be a philosopher. So I wrote a letter to all of the Fortune 500 corporations advising them of my availability for the position of company philosopher. I would be their *very* big picture man—a kind of Socratic moral gadfly pricking their corporate conscience. None of the 500 companies, however, were interested in tapping my twenty-one-year-old sense of moral superiority. Not even one.

So I became a librarian. The advantages of this choice were obvious: (1) I would always be around books; (2) I would never be put in the position of doing something of dubious morality like manufacturing napalm, disposing of toxic wastes, managing a nuclear power plant, marketing fraudulent securities, or selling defective volleyball nets; and (3) I could save the world by encouraging people to read the right books.

It never occurred to me at the time that there was any downside to becoming a librarian. I knew I would never get rich, but in the late sixties and early seventies becoming rich was not nearly as socially acceptable as it is today. In fact the thing to do at that time was to look as poor as you possibly could (even if you were rich). Wearing worn denim work shirts and tattered bell-bottom jeans showed that you were in solidarity with the oppressed and hungry people of the world.

So after one more year of college and a year of library school I became a librarian in the gritty industrial city of Hammond, Indiana, which is located about two oil slicks east of Chicago. Here the real world was very real. It was the first year of my life since I was four that I did not spend most of my waking hours in school.

For seventeen consecutive years my sense of reality had been defined by teachers, blackboards, textbooks, and final exams. For seventeen years when people asked me what I was I had always replied "student," and their reaction to this had always been positive. I was, therefore, not ready for the negative reactions that I routinely got whenever I told someone that I was a librarian.

"What are you?" people would say.

"A librarian."

"You're kidding."

"No, that's what I am."

"Oh."

The "oh" would always be accompanied by a bemused frown or a look of confusion. I quickly realized that after seventeen years of being socially acceptable, I was no longer socially acceptable. At the time this did not bother me at all because being socially acceptable was not something that I necessarily aspired to. I still carried with me a sixties sense of nonconformity: "Do your own thing and don't worry about what people think of you." If people didn't respect me for going into library work, it was their problem, not mine. I was not the least bit concerned with the attitude that real men don't go into librarianship.

But in America social values change rather quickly from one extreme to another, and predictably the celebration of nonconformity was dropped in favor of the celebration of individual success. In retrospect, this change in cultural values had something to do with the emergence of the women's movement. "You can be anything you want to be!" was what young women were now being encouraged to believe. As a result, women were now considering medical, business, legal, and even military careers. They no longer had to be nurses, teachers, or librarians. Competition for placement into law schools, medical schools, and M.B.A. programs became intense. Individual success (making money and having power), therefore, became important again not only for men, but also for women.

This left librarianship even lower than before. It now had the stigma of being a "woman's profession" that women were abandoning for more prestigious careers. What kind of man was it who would go into such a field? People assumed you were either a sissy or a wimp or probably both. Real men do heart surgery, take depositions, design buildings, and dig ditches. They do not work in libraries.

My embarrassment about being a librarian rose to the point where at all costs I would avoid any conversation about "who are you?" and "what do you do?" At times I even regretted not going into law, medicine, or ditch digging. But then I would shudder because I knew instinctively that I would not be happy doing those things. I was happy being a librarian. I loved the work. I enjoyed answering reference questions, selecting books, and running book discussions groups. There was nothing I would rather do.

But as I progressed in my career, the old issue of "real men don't go into librarianship" continued to be a problem for my ego. I bristled at the unfairness of being branded with a stereotype I didn't deserve. My salvation, of course, was in the library itself. This was my turf — the place where I was important.

Early on, in my very first library job, I noticed that very few people knew how to use the library. They needed lots of help to find what they were after. This made me an important person. I was needed, and my professional help was in demand. Inside the library not one patron ever questioned my masculinity. Outside the library people might make fun of me, but inside I was king. No, not king, more like a professor. That's how I liked to think of myself — a professor at the People's University.

Different librarians have different ways of looking at themselves. Some prefer to be thought of as information specialists, others as cultural programmers, and still others as indexers and compilers. But coming out of the populist milieu of the sixties, I have always thought of myself as an educator and the library as a free and open educational institution essential to our democratic society. To me it really is the University of the People — a school without rules, regulations, credit hours, tuition payments, diplomas, entrance exams, age requirements, transcripts, term papers, grades and final exams. It has only three entrance requirements — shoes, a shirt, and an inquiring mind. If you can meet those requirements you can go anywhere in the public library. No earthly or spiritual kingdom is too far. It's a place where you can learn how to achieve nirvana, solve a quadratic equation, fix a washing machine, and make a million dollars in the stock market.

It is also one of the most fascinating places in the entire world to work. One minute you're helping someone find a quote in the King

James Bible and the next you're breaking up a fight between two old men who are both laying claim to the Sunday edition of the *New York Times*. Despite the popular impression that librarians lead the dullest of lives, the reality is that our work is quite varied, unpredictable, and even improbable. The lack of respect that we librarians get from our fellow man is a small price to pay for being able to work each day at a job that is important, interesting, and off-beat. Whenever the thought occurs to me that I could have become a doctor, lawyer, ditch digger, senator, baseball player, or even philosopher I shudder at all the fun I would have missed hanging out at the People's U.

INDEX